PRAISE FOR DANIEL SINCLAIR

I love this book and can't imagine it being written by anyone else. Dan Sinclair is a seasoned veteran who has seen it all and had a hand in shaping the current Kingdom assault on the very ends of the Great Commission, what Jesus called "the ends of the earth." I commend this book to anyone who wants insights and practical guidance in how to turn this impossible quest into the realm of the possible.

– David Garrison, missionary author of *A Wind in the House of Islam* and *Church Planting Movements*, executive director of Global Gates

For years we have used Dan Sinclair's first book (*A Vision of the Possible*) to train new Church Planters among the unreached, and I'm excited about using this one too. I like spicy missiology and Dan is spicy – he takes some critical and controversial issues head on, makes you think, and causes you to grow. Even if you don't agree with all he says or writes, he is worth listening to and reading as his insights will both challenge and inspire you. *Mission: Possible* is both practical and powerful. I trust you will benefit from it as much as I have.

– Dick Brogden, co-Founder of the Live Dead Movement, Jeddah, Saudi Arabia

We are going to have everyone on our team and others we influence go through this book. Much like Sinclair's earlier classic, this new work is filled with pearls of truth learned through decades of ministry and communicated with wit and wisdom. Sinclair writes about apostolic calling, DMM, obedience in baptism and other ideas the missional community wrestles with in a clear articulate way that is both fun and challenging to read. The book is filled with practical advice and examples on living a healthy life focused on the most important things. He builds biblical cases that are convincing and thought provoking. It feels like you're having a conversation rather than reading a book. Hope you enjoy and grow through the lessons unleashed in this book. We truly are moving from a vision of the possible to the reality of the present where the gospel is touching the whole world. Sinclair invites his readers to be a part of this new reality.

— Rick & Megan Williams,
leaders of a large church-planting team in Saudi Arabia

Daniel Sinclair's *Mission: Possible* is a great resource for those working to reach the least reached peoples on earth. It is crammed with insight and inspiration those folks are usually craving. Daniel once asked me if I believe in Disciple Making Movements and I told him I believe in them if it is biblical discipleship. I am so grateful that in this book Daniel defines biblical discipleship in several important areas. I encourage mission practitioners and coaches to read and chew on this book.

— Dr. Don Dent, emeritus missionary,
professor of World Missions at Gateway Seminary

Approximately 30% of the world is unreached and lives without access to the Good News of Jesus. Modern missionaries have often despaired of seeing breakthroughs among Muslims, Hindus, and Buddhists. But God is doing a new thing and what has seemed impossible, God is turning into the Possible! This is not a theoretical book, but comes out of Dan Sinclair's many years in the harvest field and is a mixture of biblical examination, grappling with key issues, and real-life considerations. This is a compelling book that tells a clear story not only of what God is doing, but gives you practical and strategic ways to be involved in these modern-day miraculous "Book of Acts" movements.

— Stan Parks, PhD, movement catalyst and coach, 24:14 Coalition

I remember the days when new Christ-followers among Muslims were incredibly rare. Today, we are aware of the Holy Spirit touching many more. In this book, Dan Sinclair gives the reader practical insight into issues raised by these developments. This title is for practitioners of mission among the least reached.

– Ted Esler, PhD, president of Missio Nexus

There are not enough words to do justice to all that is in this book. This is a summary of the wisdom of a lifetime on the battlefield of Islam, an eye-witness account of astounding breakthroughs of harvesting in the Muslim world. It is also an unvarnished story of the agony of the nitty-gritty, day-to-day of facing and solving the formidable challenges that Muslim work entails. This book is filled with golden nuggets of wisdom that have come out of the testing fires of Islam. Anyone who wants to see Muslims come to Christ needs to read this veteran team leader's labor of love.

– Don McCurry, servant of Christ

In *Mission: Possible* Daniel Sinclair has provided us with a great store of practical wisdom and Biblical insights to help those serving God cross-culturally. It combines apostolic passion, helpful analysis of Disciple Making Movements, and lessons for practical life and ministry. I warmly recommend this book.

– David Devenish, Newfrontiers Together Team

As a practitioner with many years of field experience living among Muslims in the Middle East, as a coach who has mentored numerous teams to bring in the harvest, as a strategist who tried both a traditional approach to church planting and then humbly retooled to catalyze movements, and as a brother whose soul is well nourished by the Word of God, Sinclair brings a wealth of experience to those of us longing to see Jesus treasured among the family of Ishmael. If you are about to head to the field or you need a reboot after years on the field, this book is for you.

– Nathan Lutz, founder of TOAG internships and trainer with Frontiers

At the beginning of the 90s, my family and I started our missionary service in the Muslim world, having Costa Rica as our sending base. During that season, I meet Dan Sinclair and many of his colleagues at Frontiers. I vividly remember their passionate reports on their progress through the *Seven Church-Planting Phases*. Twenty-five years later, we are not only talking about evangelism and Church planting; today, we witness a growing movement of Muslims coming to Jesus. We live in a new season, expecting more to come! With this journey in mind, I celebrate the publication of Dan's book, *Mission: Possible*, a stimulating toolbox that masterly combines the Bible, a historical understanding, and practical tools on DMM and church multiplication. May the Lord bring more movements among the Unreached still needing to hear and respond to the good news of Jesus Christ! ¡Muchas Gracias Dan!

– Allan E. Matamoros, North Africa & Middle East Director
Partners International, COMIBAM Field Director,
chairman of the Vision 5:9 Network.

Imagine sitting down with a veteran missionary and allowing him to share what he has learned through years of service. That is what this book is all about. It touches on many topics relevant to today's modern missionary situation. It contains such good advice that I found myself writing down notes and tips that I want to apply to my own life. All in all, I found this book to be a great personal encouragement and I will be sure to recommend it to all my teammates.

– Roland Muller, author of *Honor & Shame*
and *The Messenger, the Message, and the Community*

My prayer for the missionaries who read this superb book is, "O God, let them be fruitful so that thousands and millions of non-Christians will "glorify You for Your mercy." For praying Christians who want to learn from one of the most Biblical teachers I have known, you will be rewarded by reading this book. For Christian leaders, who want guidance in your ministry of sending missionaries, here is wise counsel from one who has been doing the work of the evangelist for more than 30 years. For the critic, who has decided that "movement thinking" is not Biblical, it is time to find out where you got that idea. For the author, Dan Sinclair, my lifelong friend, now is time for all Christians to return to the Bible to go forward to the final mission frontiers.

– Robert A. Blincoe, PhD, president emeritus of Frontiers

There is real treasure here! Over the years of faithful pursuit of making Jesus known among the unreached, it is like the author has mined a vein of gold through his experience of success, failure, perseverance, tears and hard work and in these pages sets it out as practical life lessons for the benefit of others. There is wisdom here for anyone involved in cross cultural ministry—read it, digest it, pray and then put it into practice, you and those around you will benefit.

– Andy Martin, Newfrontiers, church planter and coach who has been involved in Muslim-world ministry for 20 years

For nearly 40 years, Dan Sinclair has been an on-the-ground participant as well as a keen observer of what God has been doing among Muslims worldwide. In this well-written and highly informative new book, Sinclair takes the reader through his journey from focusing on the planting of individual fellowships to seeing networks or movements of new disciples of Jesus take shape among Muslims. Aware of the great differences that exist among Muslims worldwide, Sinclair acknowledges that the forms disciple-making movements take will vary widely, depending on particular Muslim peoples and cultures.

– John Jay Travis, PhD, author and affiliate professor at Fuller Theological Seminary
– Anna Travis, MA, author and consultant in intercultural studies

The Sinclairs are the best of mentors and friends, and our lives wouldn't be the same without them. They had a role in bringing us together in marriage, in getting us "out the door" to China, and in keeping us standing firm over the many years of ministry. We highly endorse them--and anything they may write.

– Nicholas and Denele Ivins, needy fellow servants of Christ

MISSION: POSSIBLE

DEFINING AND EMPOWERING YOUR MINISTRY AMONG THE UNREACHED

DANIEL SINCLAIR

Foreword by
GREG LIVINGSTONE

MOF PUBLISHING

Copyright © 2021 by Daniel Sinclair

All rights reserved.

No part of this book may be reproduced in any form or by any electronic or mechanical means, including information storage and retrieval systems, without written permission from the author, except for the use of brief quotations in a book review.

Scripture quotations are from the ESV® Bible (The Holy Bible, English Standard Version®), copyright © 2001 by Crossway, a publishing ministry of Good News Publishers. Used by permission. All rights reserved. May not copy or download more than 500 consecutive verses of the ESV Bible or more than one half of any book of the ESV Bible.

ISBN 978-0-9958951-9-5 (print); 978-1-7776615-0-2 (e-book)

Published by MOF Publishing; mofpublishing@proinbox.com; mofpublishing.com

CONTENTS

Foreword	xi
Introduction	xiii
1. Apostleship Revisited	1
2. The Case for Counting	31
3. Baptism in Resistant Cultures	39
4. DMM for Dummies	51
5. Time Stewardship on the Field	87
Appendix 1: Movements Around the World	149
Appendix 2: Apostleship FAQs	159
Appendix 3: Jesus' Sending Out the 12 and the 72	171
Appendix 4: Examples of Shema Statements	173
Appendix 5: A Typical DBS Meeting	175
Appendix 6: Sample of DBS Lesson Sets	177
Appendix 7: The Story of Alma	179
Appendix 8: Handling Lots of Email	183
Bibliography	187
Special Thanks	193

FOREWORD

There's almost nothing theoretical about Dan, a coach who gives you his best stuff. If you're into American football, Dan is the Bill Belichick of the greatest rescue mission in history—the challenge of turning from death to life the billions still in resistant populations, still imprisoned in the Enemy's deceptions. If you don't know Belichick, he's the winningest coach in the history of American football.

So VERY grateful for Dan's first book, *A Vision of the Possible: Pioneer Church Planting in Teams*, and how that got the vital message to teams led by the apostolically gifted and motivated.

Dan is a coach who's "been there, done that" and pretty much seen it all, night and day, for over 25 years! What he writes is not meant to be erudite—it's meant to be a playbook of the fundamentals. What he coaches in *Mission: Possible* is coming from a coach who deeply wants you, in your generation, to win!

In our case, that means pioneering efforts among those who are tragically still on the road that leads to the resurrection of judgment (see John 5:29). That's what apostolic mission is!

If you're on God's team, involved in HIS rescue operation, you've already devoured Dan's first book *A Vision of the Possible*.

But Dan, since writing that, has winced; yes and even wept, as a Field Director of Frontiers, hurting with those who have been "struck down, if not out."

In his latest book he is providing MORE detailed coaching to bolster pioneer (apostolic) disciple-makers "where Christ is not acknowledged" as the Savior, Romans 15:20.

The principles and practices illustrated, in detail, in *Mission: Possible* all reflect the furnace of ministering where we are not wanted; where many missionaries have "turned back" due to a lack of this kind of coaching; where every generation of the Lord's apostles/pioneer missionaries have been considered, in Paul's words, "the scum of the earth."

Arabic-speaking Dan has been in the thick of church planting efforts—while living in the Middle East—coming alongside and assisting those who experienced everything that could go wrong. He's also journeyed with those whose efforts in practicing the wisdom in this book meant they overcame, endured, and left behind rescued people with whom we will spend eternity!

On these vital subjects, there is no one else's writing I'd rather endorse (well, Piper's probably).

Devour this great coaching,

Dr. Greg Livingstone

Founder, Frontiers

P.S. Dan and his sparky wife gave me my first challenge to found Frontiers.

INTRODUCTION

This is an odd book. On the one hand, there are missiological and inspiring parts, like Chapter 1 about apostleship and Kingdom advance worldwide. And there are instructional sections like Chapter 4, a practical thumbnail sketch concerning **movements** ministry. But how does Chapter 5 about time stewardship fit in? I guess I've always felt that when workers discuss ministry without also contending with practical, everyday, rubber-meets-the-road personal issues, then something is lacking. By combining the two (chapters 1–4 with chapter 5), it is my hope that you find this book both inspiring and practical.

This book follows on from *A Vision of the Possible: Pioneer Church Planting in Teams*,[1] which first came out in 2006, and was aimed primarily at frontline workers. Imagine my astonishment when it sold around 25,000 copies, in three languages. More importantly were the many stories that poured in telling how God was using it to enhance field ministries. Both the first book and this new one center around the exciting New Testament dynamic of apostleship.

Taking the gospel to peoples who have never heard, among whom there is yet no body of disciples, is the essence of apostleship. With an appreciation of biblical apostleship, we are better able to keep this spiritual entrepreneurship and pioneering front and center—which can be crucial when the going gets tough out there. Think about it: If you are about to move your family to a very foreign and maybe dangerous place on the globe, how important is your purpose and motivation? Are you going just because a missions brochure caught your eye? That a slogan resonated with you? That you got stirred up during Brother So-and-So's inspirational message? Or maybe your church has so normalized going (a good thing) that young people who lack direction just line up saying, "Here am I", maybe to have an experience overseas, but perhaps with unclear motives. All these things can play a part in the process in deciding to sign up. But you should only go if you genuinely believe that what you are doing is solidly biblical, that it is how you can serve the Lord well with your life, and that it fits in with two millennia of precedent of men and women going out **to where Christ is not known**.

We're talking high-stakes life and ministry here. And there are no guarantees. You may not see much visibly accomplished over many years, you or your family members may suffer much or even lose your lives. Or, as many have over the centuries, you may play a part in changing the spiritual landscape of a whole country for generations. Some actually do both: They don't see much direct fruit, but soon after they leave, the seeds of the gospel begin to bring great fruit, in part because of the faithful soil tilling and seed planting of those early workers. One can look to such movements in China, Korea, and Iran, where visible fruit was slow to come but where the Church is now enormous to the glory of Christ. We can be 110% confident that all of this is possible because the gospel can go from **zero to movements** because of God's design for apostolic ministry.

In the mid-1980s a fresh new emphasis on **church-planting** and **unreached people groups (UPGs)** was taking hold. This is not to say that these were new ideas—certainly not. But what was new was the momentum, the numbers of people who wanted to go to the field in frontier ways, and new creative sending structures that were established. The idea of the **10/40 Window**[2]—and Muslim peoples in particular—awakened people's attention in the church and in missions and convinced us that this was from God. Dozens, and eventually hundreds, of new teams sprung up and went out to some of the most unreached peoples and neglected cities in the world. But no one then, that I am aware of, was connecting the dots with the New Testament notion of **apostleship**. Soon that would change.

Something unusual began to happen in the late-1990s, sort of like unexpected wildflowers appearing after a rain. Several individuals, unconnected with each other and scattered around the globe, began to be intrigued by the same subject. We were discovering how certain New Testament words held much power as they described our calling: **the work** (in the Greek *ton ergon*), **fellow workers** (*sunergoi*), **apostle** (*apostolos*), and **apostleship** (*apostolé*).

I cannot imagine a more fulfilling time than today to be engaged in pioneer movements and church-planting ministry. There is still so very much more work to do. Nonetheless, there have been **far more** movements among unreached peoples (such as Muslims, Hindus, Buddhists) since 2000 AD than all previous centuries combined. Fasten your seatbelts as you read Chapter 1 ("Apostleship Revisited") and Appendix 1 ("Movements around the World").

A Vision of the Possible was penned mostly in 2004, and as the title suggests, it was more about envisioning what was coming and preparing for it. In our organization, at least, we had not yet witnessed a big upturn in visible results on the fields. Soon afterward, we did. *Mission: Possible* continues the themes but grapples more practically with advanced issues of Harvest.

The astute reader will notice that illustrations from Muslim contexts outnumber those from other contexts. For those of you working among other UPGs, my apologies! It is simply that I have more experience from the former, but surely this book is just as much for you.

Throughout this book, I refer to **Disciple-Making Movements** or **DMM**. Unfortunately to some people, this may connote a particular methodology or **brand** of movement-oriented ministry, which is not my intent. It's just that "DMM" is now often used as a generic term for **church-planting movement** approaches.[3] For example, Chapter 4 is entitled "DMM for Dummies." But surely you can understand how

"Movement Approaches to Church Planting for Dummies" wouldn't have the same panache.

So Chapters 1–4 concern missiology and practical how-tos of ministry, whereas Chapter 5 addresses how we can personally best steward our time, describing eight life skills—a bit of a switch. For this reason, the reader may wish to begin reading Chapter 1, and then switch over to Chapter 5, taking in its introduction and Life Skill #1. The reader could continue to alternate between Chapters 1–4 and Chapter 5. Just a suggestion that might make it even more practical.

Finally, every writer of non-fiction wrestles with deciding what should be a chapter and what might serve better as an appendix. All of the appendices are hopefully very relevant. And I would especially urge you not to miss Appendices 1 ("Movements around the World"), 2 ("Apostleship FAQs"), and 7 ("The Story of Alma").

Daniel Sinclair

Middle East

2021

---

1. Sinclair, Daniel. *A Vision of the Possible: Pioneer Church Planting in Teams.* Downers Grove, IL: IVP books 2005.
2. "The 10/40 Window is the rectangular area of North Africa, the Middle East and Asia approximately between 10 degrees north and 40 degrees north latitude. The 10/40 Window is often called "The Resistant Belt" and includes the majority of the world's Muslims, Hindus, and Buddhists." https://joshuaproject.net
3. Sort of like "Kleenex" for all facial tissues, I guess.

1

APOSTLESHIP REVISITED

Why this major New Testament theme remains THE key issue for work among the unreached

"Paul, a servant of Christ Jesus, called to be an apostle, set apart for the gospel of God... Through [Jesus] we have received grace and apostleship to bring about the obedience of faith for the sake of his name among all the nations, including you... in Rome."

- Paul, introducing himself to the church in Rome, whom he had not yet met, (Romans 1:1-7)

"...many persons of every age, every rank, and also of both sexes are and will be endangered. For the contagion of this superstition has spread not only to the cities but also to the villages and farms."

- Pliny, governor of the distant province of Bithynia, warning Emperor Trajan about Christians (ca. AD 111)

MISSION: POSSIBLE

> *"We are but of yesterday, and yet we have filled all the places that belong to you — cities, islands, forts, towns, exchanges, the military camps themselves, tribes, town councils, the palace, the senate, the market-place; we have left you nothing but your temples."*
>
> - Tertullian (late 2nd century) to his Roman persecutors (in *Plea for Allegiance*)

Adoniram Judson entered Burma (now known as Myanmar) in July 1813. He went to India first where William Carey told him not to go. It was too dangerous. There was war with Siam (now Thailand), raids, rebellion and no religious freedom. All the missionaries had died or left.

Judson went anyway. He was 24; his wife was 23. Their first three children died—the first stillborn on the boat between India and Burma; the second died after 17 months; the third died at two, only six months after her mother died. Judson lost three children and his wife in his first years in Burma.

He was thrown in prison. His legs fettered. At night a bamboo pole was inserted in his leg chains and lifted up, so that all night long, his feet were in the air and only his head and shoulders could touch the dirty ground. He slept this way every night for 17 months. He was marched through the jungle barefoot, emaciated, sick and weak.

Imprisoned with an unbelieving European, Judson was mocked: 'What think ye now of the prospects that any Burmese will be converted?' Picture this with me. Judson in ragged and dirty clothes, scarred feet and chain-chaffed ankles, feet in the air, sweat on his brow, replied, 'The prospects are as bright as the promises of God!'

He remarried and his second wife died. He remarried and his third wife also died. His brother died. His father died. Another child died. Judson knew great suffering and was bruised by much death. After 10 years, there were only 18 converts in the church.

However, by the year 2000, because of Judson's work to preach the gospel and translate the Scriptures, because of his 'White Martyrdom,' the Baptist convention in Myanmar consisted of 3,700 churches,

617,781 members, and 1,900,000 affiliates. Judson was a grain of wheat that fell to the ground and died.[1]

Such is not new. The cost of pioneer missionary work is often high. Several years ago, my wife and I visited a team in a remote town in South Asia, in a country impacted by war and jihadism. Despite the hardships and dangers, they were doing wonderfully at learning the language and culture, having lots of friendships and building a solid reputation, and serving the people through a humanitarian project. The team was, and still is, sharing Christ with people regularly. There were a couple of local believers, but the gospel work was slow and often discouraging.

On this visit we agreed it would be good for me to buy a *shalwar-kameez*, as I was about the only male in the entire town wearing western clothes. Nigel, the team leader, asked the neighbor boy to take me to the *souq*. Habibullah was a delightful sixteen-year-old and was very helpful. It took a while for us to find my size, since I'm bigger than most locals.

Two weeks after we had returned home to England, we got an urgent call from the team: Habibullah had been shot dead, and Nigel was in jail charged with his murder. An unknown assailant had been up on the outer wall late at night and had fired into Nigel's yard. Habibullah's father and family lived next door, and the two families shared the common back garden. He must have been outside with the animals and was shot in the back, and the shooter likely thought he was shooting Nigel. We deeply grieved for the dear boy and his family.

We dropped everything to do whatever we could to coordinate with others on Nigel's behalf. Over the next two weeks, a steady flow of captured jihadists came and went, held in the jail cells next to Nigel. Included among them were two young men from Nigel's neighborhood, whom Nigel was told were hauled in on suspicion of involvement in Habibullah's murder. Needless to say, it was very disconcerting for Nigel to have them just inches away, in the cell right next to him, whispering menacingly back and forth.

After 15 days Nigel was told he would be released from prison if he quietly left the city. With great sadness and reluctance, the family left the people they had loved. A couple of days later we picked them up at Heathrow. After a brief time back in the US the family returned to the region to continue their work with the same people group in a neighboring country. The previous team continues to press on to this day, and are encouraged, though there is not yet a significant breakout of the gospel.

Here's the point: This family were faithful to their calling. But in God's sovereign plan, even in that calling, they suffered danger and a tragic crisis, and didn't see much fruit. They pressed on anyway in another location, trusting God's good plans for the people group on their hearts. Passion. Sacrifice. Willingness to suffer. And a holy discontent and restlessness to see Christ's purposes accomplished.

Elsewhere, a friend and colleague writes how they were so blessed to see the whole church-planting cycle take place in Kazakhstan, like in the book of Acts:

> What was thrilling and humbling was to be honored as the apostles (founders) of this church. Many fellow pastors came from all over the country to be part of the celebration and encourage them. But they gave us special honor as part of the very first missionary group to bring the gospel to their totally unreached part of the world. It brings tears to my eyes to think that I have had a small part in the gospel breaking through and the church being established in this difficult, Muslim area of the world. They had prepared a slide show and there we were, 15 years ago, living with them in the village. It was amazing to think how far we have all come in the Lord since then. They started out as baby Christians and we as the church planters, and now we are peers doing church planting together![2]

What do these three stories have in common? Almost everything. All of these families and their teammates were called by Christ into apostolic ministry—to take the gospel and seek to plant churches among those who have never heard, going where the spiritual needs are greatest, accepting their respective assignments. All were faithful, gifted, operating in the Spirit's power, and were laboring in order to see the whole spiritual landscape of the country or people group changed for Christ. The Kazakhstan team saw happy results during their time. That South Asia team has not yet seen much fruit but press on anyway. And from the Judson ministry in Myanmar has come tremendous fruit for Christ and the growth of His church there. But Adoniram Judson and his wives never saw any of that during their lifetimes and endured much affliction in their calling. No doubt all these will hear that, "Well done, good and faithful servant. You have been faithful over a little; I will set you over much. Enter into the joy of your master."[3] None of these will have any regrets. It is not trite when we say that we leave the results to God. We mean it.

Significant harvest among unreached people groups is not merely possible, but is, in fact, happening all around the world. We have in the rest of this chapter significant support from the Bible for what is being asserted, some practical contemporary application points, and finally a brief sampling of some incredible developments around the globe. If you must jump to that last section, go to "It's Not Just 'Possible,' but is Happening!" But promise me you'll go back and read what you skipped. OK?

There is also "Apostleship FAQs" (Appendix 2).

Why Does It Matter Anyway?

The quotes at the beginning from Pliny and Tertullian demonstrate how the gospel burst across the known world in the first two centuries of the Church. Not only were churches established all over the Middle East, Europe, and North Africa, but even outside the Roman Empire to Persia, Central Asia (the "-stans" today) and beginning to move into China. Despite what we sometimes read, this progress actually began to slow down considerably after the Edict of Milan in 313 AD, when Constantine gave legal status to Christianity. Could the initial 120 believers on the day of Pentecost have ever imagined that things would expand so incredibly? And what accounts for this wide and unstoppable momentum? I suggest to you two factors:

- Every time a new church was founded, the believers' lives were transformed, and they were serious about following their newfound Savior. As we read in the book of Revelation: *"And they have conquered him by the blood of the Lamb and by the word of their testimony, for they loved not their lives even unto death."* (12:11)
- From the earliest days of the Church, there was an understanding of and energetic support for **apostolic ministry**. With each advance, some would step forward to say, "I want to give my life to go out to cities and peoples who have not yet heard," and the church would get behind them.

It was a chilly January 1 morning, in the early 1980s, when our family first arrived in our new home in Egypt. The evening before, sitting at the gate at New York's JFK, felt like waiting to depart Planet Earth on a mission to Mars.

Let's face it: Anyone who would leave family and friends; a good job; a home; one's own country, culture, and language; and move to the other side of the world where everything is so different and scary and economically poorer—not to mention hostile to the message—must be a little nuts, right? Numerous other times I've been asked, "So you guys must really like it over there, right?" expecting to hear the affirmative. After all, the reasons for going must be the adventure, the stimulation from other cultures, foreign travel, and the like. Not!

If you're a worker in a foreign country, laboring to bring Christ to an unreached people group, I'm sure you've experienced the same. The reason we seem to be such oddballs is that our calling is different. There's only one reason to do what we're doing: because Christ wants us to do it. Why? Because God loves all people, not just us.

Paul's consciousness of being called as an apostle had a profound impact on his life and ministry. Nothing would ever again be the same. First of all, he knew that his gospel ministry was not his whim, idea, or chosen career path. Rather, it came from God's initiative. Therefore, it came with God's authority. Paul often reminded people, in the churches which he had started, of his apostleship—and of his awareness that God was communicating to them **through him**!

Secondly, Paul's awareness of calling eliminated any shrinking back from discharging his ministry with all faithfulness, whatever the cost. "For if I preach the gospel, I have nothing to boast of, for **I am under compulsion; for woe is me if I do not preach the gospel**. For if I do this voluntarily, I have a reward; but if against my will, **I have a stewardship entrusted to me**" (1 Corinthians 9:16-17; NASB; emphasis added). This "stewardship," of course, was his apostolic ministry. As Paul said in his emotional farewell to the elders of the church at Ephesus, "I do not consider my life of any account as dear to myself, so that I may finish my course and **the ministry which I received from the Lord Jesus**" (Acts 20:24; emphasis added). One team leader confided in me, "Paul's sense of apostolic call has had a profound effect on me and my ministry, Dan, forcing me to plead with Christ Jesus constantly to grant me His grace that I might be faithful until the end, not turning to the right or the left in my vocational and ministerial aspirations. I am a bond slave of Christ, called to die to my own will and live for His alone."[4]

With some things in life, getting the fundamentals right instead of wrong can make all the difference in the world. Consider this example from the field of investing:

> Measure twice, cut once. If there is one company that suddenly everyone knows, it is Zoom, the videoconferencing company. It's a great product, and the stock (ticker symbol ZM) has enjoyed strong gains this year—up 123%. But there's another Zoom that has done even better. It's an obscure Chinese company with no revenue that happens to be listed on the U.S. market, and with a much better ticker symbol: ZOOM. As a result, this other Zoom's stock, which in the past typically traded for about a penny a share, has shot up nearly 900% this year. The lesson: If you're making changes to your portfolio in this environment, go slow and be careful of making decisions under stress.[5]

We must likewise get a handle on the nature of biblical pioneering ministry as we launch out ourselves or send others out.

Picture this: a middle-aged missionary arrives alone in a large city where Christ followers are considered 'heathen' because they reject the local gods. As far as he's aware, among the hundreds of thousands of the population, there are absolutely zero believers. This prosperous port city is famous for their immorality and the love of the people to philosophize about life and the supernatural. Previously it had been known as quite the center for sports, especially professional boxing. Though their language is not his mother-tongue, he doesn't need to engage in language studies, since he has a pretty good grasp of the *lingua franca*. He gets a place to stay, and spends the days walking around, observing and praying, while he awaits the arrival of some teammates, who had been delayed. Is he intimidated and stressed? No, he is energized. This is wide open territory where Christ is unknown, and he's confident that the Holy Spirit will cause a number of households to enter the Kingdom as a result of his visit!

After a week or so he sets up his work stall, to hand-sew and sell various models of outdoor shelter. Soon he meets another **outsider** couple making tents, and it turns out they're also believers! They decide to team up in ministry. Before long many in this major Greek city follow Christ and things take off. You see, the missionary is Paul, and the city is Corinth. This sort of intention and going and counting on God to open doors has been repeated thousands of times over the centuries.

We may often feel like failures. So, let's remind ourselves that there simply is no more significant human activity in the present course of human events. Would you rather be a rock star? A really rich guy? A high-flying business executive? A quarterback with a Super Bowl ring? Ha! Why exchange your rich calling for a bowl of porridge?

What Does the New Testament Teach?

Before we return to specific applications of biblical apostleship, let's spend a few pages on nuances of New Testament teaching. Please stay with me here. You will see that ultimately these issues are not just foundational, but exciting in their implications. There is an immense sustaining impact on our lives when we take the time to draw our convictions from the Word. Amen?

The Four+ Times Jesus Gave the Great Commission

I used to think to myself that since missions work can be so complex or confusing, that it sure would have been helpful if the Lord had left us with a **job description**. Then one day I realized that He had! No missions conference would be complete without someone teaching on **The Great Commission** in Matthew 28:18-20, and we'll look at that in a bit of detail in a moment.

This Mandate was so crucial in the ultimate purposes of our Lord that He articulated it on at least four occasions, in varying ways, after His Resurrection and up to His Ascension:

1. Matthew 28:18-20 *"All authority in heaven and on earth has been given to me. Go therefore and make disciples of all nations, baptizing them in the name of the Father and of the Son and of the Holy Spirit, teaching them to observe all that I have commanded you. And behold, I am with you always, to the end of the age."*

2. Mark 16:15 (same event as Matthew 28) *"Go into all the world and proclaim the gospel to the whole creation."*

3. Luke 24:46-47 *"Thus it is written, that the Christ should suffer and on the third day rise from the dead, and that repentance and forgiveness of sins should be proclaimed in his name to all nations, beginning from Jerusalem."*

4. John 20:21 *"Peace be with you. As the Father has sent me, even so I am sending you."*

5. Acts 1:8 *"But you will receive power when the Holy Spirit has come upon you, and you will be my witnesses in Jerusalem and in all Judea and Samaria, and to the end of the earth."*

It's thrilling down to our toes to truly grasp the scope of all these: **all nations (twice), all the world, the whole creation, and to the end of the earth**. As if that weren't enough, John 20:21 caps it: the mandate from God the Father to God the Son, i.e. His redemptive purposes for the entire human race, are now transferred to us. Gulp.

Senders and Goers

We know that Jesus wants to use all believers in His purposes, locally and globally. As Paul says, *"For we are his workmanship, created in Christ Jesus for good works, which God prepared beforehand, that we should walk in them."* (Ephesians 2:10) What an enormous privilege! No one is sidelined. And in light of John 20:21 above, even His worldwide **sending** is in some way for all.

And let us not forget this special dynamic: *"The one who receives a prophet because he is a prophet will receive a prophet's reward, and the one who receives a righteous person because he is a righteous person will receive a righteous person's reward. And whoever gives one of these little ones even a cup of cold water because he is a disciple, truly, I say to you, he will by no means lose his reward."* (Matthew 10:41-42) Jesus is telling us that we can meaningfully participate in other believers' works by helping and reinforcing them. So I can partner with another's ministry in Boise or Botswana through prayer, finances, learning, logistics or other practical supports. I then have a share in the outcomes too.

Finally, on the senders side of things, we observe in Romans 15:22-32 how Paul appeals for the whole church at Rome to assist in his envisioned ministry to Spain, both in finances and in prayer. When my wife and I write to our prayer and financial supporters, and to our Senders Team, it can sometimes feel cliché to always say how grateful we are for their *partnership* with us. But we mean it genuinely from our hearts. Goers can't do what they do without Senders doing what they do. The role of the local church and of Senders particularly in changing the world is indeed very great!

But Let's Not Lose the Uniqueness of This Calling

As mentioned, I believe Jesus' directive to the Eleven recorded in Matthew 28:19-20 and Mark 16:15 is a kind of **job description** for all engaged in apostolic ministry. But Houston we have a problem. Are the specifics of this for all believers, everywhere and in all times? On the one hand, certainly all believers can be involved in making disciples, conveying Jesus' teaching and urging obedience to His commands, and evangelism/baptizing—laboring to build up Christ's Body. And as we just saw, the role of Senders in global outreach is 110% vital. But are ALL supposed to ACTUALLY GO, i.e. move away from their literal home to preach the gospel?

I'm convinced that the answer is no, and this should be an encouragement to both Senders and Goers. Why is this so?

- It's definitely a command to 'Go'. While the verb form is a participle, there are ironclad reasons why every major translation translates it as a command (imperative).[6] To translate it as "As you go" or "While going (wherever you happen to be)" is simply bad Greek. And we absolutely mustn't water down this crucial command for <u>some</u> to actually GO.
- The direct recipients of the Matthew, Mark, Luke and Acts renderings of this mandate were all explicitly to the Eleven apostles. He absolutely wanted these men (and families where applicable) to GO. And they did. Though for a decade or two they focused their ministry on the Jews,[7] eventually all of the Twelve (the Eleven plus Mathias) labored heroically to far-flung nations. It's really incredible how these 12 leaders, under the Lord's commission, took the gospel all across the Middle East, Iran, Egypt, Africa, India, Central Asia and the Caucuses, and even extending into Europe, including Britain.[8] In doing so, they all died martyrs' deaths, with the possible exception of John. We recall that the book of the "Acts of the Apostles" is the story of apostolic teams GOING out to the nations. They were fulfilling the Apostolic Directive, aka the Great Commission. Then in the book of Acts and rest of the New Testament the mandate

expands to many more small 'a' apostles and fellow-workers, who were also to actually leave home and go out to the nations, because of their calling to apostleship, which in Romans 1:5 Paul calls 'grace,' i.e. an enormous privilege.
- If we interpret Matthew 28:19, et al., as meaning Jesus wants all sincere Christians to head out to other lands and peoples, thus being missionaries, then 99.9% of the church is in disobedience. I recently heard a sermon that pretty much said just that. It was in a safe **missionary** setting. I'm like, "Dude. You can't say that!" The truth is, no one in the New Testament is ever chided for not leaving home for the sake of the gospel. Guilt trips on all non-goers is simply not biblical.
- The apostolic calling and task are very unique and special—not in an exalted way, but in a sobering way.

Can you see the fine line I'm trying to walk here? At the very least, we must recognize that there is particular applicability of this Great Commission to those called to apostolic ministry.

A Unique Calling, You Say?

Note the distinction Paul makes in 2 Corinthians 4:12: "So death is at work in us, but life in you." The "death" is the grueling experiences of apostles he just described in vv 5-11. And the "life" is the new life and resurrection power new believers come into as churches are planted. Of course, elsewhere he also speaks about how all believers are subject to persecution and suffering. Nonetheless, we also read him describing the unique and often painful experiences of apostles in 1 Corinthians 4:9-13. Throughout history and today so many in apostolic ministry really do feel at times like "the scum of the world, the refuse of all things," especially when opposition to their message becomes severe. "The upside for Paul— that God's chosen people in each place might find salvation—far outweighed the downside of enduring ridicule, beatings, imprisonment, shipwrecks and stoning."[9] A friend of mine was strung up by a mob with a rope around his neck in West Africa. If the police had arrived on the scene just a moment later, he would have been hanged. So, if you are thus engaged, aren't you glad you're so **special**?

Another friend puts it this way: "God calls us to count the cost. Before moving overseas, we try to count the cost. But the cost keeps changing! We agree to the cost before we can ever know what it is. It's like signing a book of blank checks from our personal bank account, and then handing the checks over to the Lord. He fills in the amounts and the dates. But no matter what the cost is, He makes sure that we have the balance in our accounts. He is faithful." Are you **cut out** for this? Most of us aren't. But we are **being cut out** along the way, and that's OK.

Speaking of the cost, in our organization we've seen people beaten almost to death, one shot to death in front of his son, some who had to clean up after dear fellow workers were killed for their testimony, those imprisoned, those having children die from terrible accidents on the field, death threats beyond counting, a wife being made a widow with four small children to raise, a number die from odd diseases and leave grieving families behind, one suffering a car accident leaving him paralyzed for life—brothers and sisters of whom this world is not worthy—not to speak of the daily hardships of life in some very hard places. The Celtic Church spoke of Green martyrs—those who lived but denied themselves the safety which would assure their living to old age, and the Red martyrs, who gave the last full measure of devotion to their Savior.[10] Of course, apostolic workers do not have a monopoly on such suffering, as persecution on believers endured in emerging churches can be as bad or worse.

Let's also not forget that oftentimes there is special protection too. For example, Brad and Karen were gospel workers in a town in Oman well known for its deep involvement in the occult. After a while they began to experience strange happenings in the home, such as demons impersonating their voices. So, they decided to go room-by-room and spiritually sanitize the whole house, praying and anointing parts with oil. The strange occurrences ceased. A few weeks later Karen's Omani friends asked her, "Why is it, Karen, that the spirits that we see around your house now only sit on the wall, and seem not permitted to go near your house?" Brad later wrote, "Our prayers in the name of Jesus turned off the poltergeist-type phenomena like turning off a faucet."

Us Oddballs[11]

Finally, have you ever noticed how sometimes missionaries or pre-field goers can seem like odd ducks, hearing the beat of a different drummer, not quite fitting in at church? I love this testimony from Neal, a good friend of mine, about how the process of apostolic calling eventually took over his life. He and his wife and kids have labored very effectively in several countries among those who have never heard. And today Neal gives training in Disciple Making Movements (see Chapter 4) to hundreds of expat workers, Arab Christians, and Muslim-background believers, resulting in a couple very large movements:

> I do believe that God has gifted me with the apostleship. I don't claim to have always been a wise steward of that gift. Nevertheless, I'd be blind if I didn't see it in my life.
>
> I did not grow up bold. I have never been extroverted. I didn't do sleepovers with friends. I didn't go on school camps. I wasn't involved in church groups. I didn't travel to other countries. I had no interest in such things. I stayed close to home. It was what I knew and was comfortable with. During my senior year of high school, a gal challenged me to read about the life of Jesus. To try to win favor with her, I did. My life forever changed. For months I worked my way through the Scriptures with the Spirit of God changing me. I was not going to any church at the time, but about four months into the journey I began *cautiously* attending a church.
>
> I connected with the pastor, and he invested into me. Mind you, I was not yet a believer, though I continued to read through the Scriptures. And about nine months after starting to read, I decided to believe and get baptized. I felt like a new baby in the world. I was a brand, new believer with virtually no church background. I felt that I had so much to learn and was so eager to just devote myself to learning and growing.
>
> One week after getting baptized, I drove through a part of town and didn't see any churches at all. So, I turned around and drove to my church and met with my pastor. I thanked him for investing in me but told him that I was going to leave the church. Shocked he asked me why.

I told him about this part of town that had no churches and thus I presumed no believers, and so I decided that I was going to go there and start a church. I had no idea what that meant. But it seemed what I was being compelled to do. The pastor told me that I might need more than a week of being a believer to attempt such a task and might need some more time to grow. He then paired me with a mature believer a few years older than me. Together we started a discipleship group and started reaching non-believers. It was awesome, but after a few months this beloved mentor began to show me God's heart for the nations from the Bible. So, I found myself quickly telling my friend that based on this I was going to move overseas. He was shocked. He asked me where I was going and I responded, "I need to know that?" He then asked me when I was going, and I too responded, "I need to know that also?"

I remember telling him that I didn't know, but I was going. Because that is what I felt compelled to do. It is what God said to do.

For those who knew me growing up, none of this made sense. I was not the adventurous outgoing type. I stayed at home. I didn't like people that were different than me. But all that changed when I committed my life to Jesus. A new Spirit and purpose began to reside within me. No one ever labeled it. No one told me to do it. I just did it. It wasn't until probably ten years later that I even began to connect all these dots to see that it was a perfect match for the biblical small "a" calling of apostleship. Just no one around me had ever used that terminology. As a matter of fact, I kind of felt a bit out of place often in the church, though I loved it and served in it, and I struggled to just be content ministering to believers or even new visitors. Many others seemed perfectly fine with that—I wasn't. The dissonance began to grow.[12]

Paul's Letter to the Church in Rome Redux: The 1 to 15 Connection

It's clear in Romans 1:1-5 (see the epigraph at the beginning of the chapter) that right out of the gate Paul wants his readers and future ministry partners in Rome to accept him being an apostle and getting a good grasp concerning his ministry of apostleship. And he unabashedly declares in 11:3: *"Now I am speaking to you Gentiles. Inasmuch then as I am an apostle to the Gentiles, I magnify my ministry..."* It's odd then that when he unpacks what all this means in chapter 15, and again invites their financial and other help toward his envisioned western Mediterranean campaign,[13] he doesn't use the a-word. In 15:16-23 we find such a succinct and powerful description of what apostolic teams do in going to the unreached. [This is a text that should be preached in every church in the world at least annually.] He again sets aside any false humility to promote his ministry—though he's clear that it is all God's doing rather than personal achievement. *Pioneering* ministry is not a new word or concept vis. apostleship.

Now this is interesting: We discover that 15:18 especially links back to 1:5:

- 1:5 *through whom we have received grace and apostleship to bring about the obedience of faith for the sake of his name among all the nations;*
- 15:18 *For I will not venture to speak of anything except what Christ has accomplished through me to bring the Gentiles to obedience.*

Four things provide us an unmistakable link between the two texts. First is "the obedience of the Gentiles/nations"—same words in the Greek. Second, in 15:15 he again picks up the theme of **the grace given me by God**, i.e. the rich privilege of his calling and ministry, as in 1:5. And because this calling is to all the Gentiles/nations, he must now head to Spain, since his unique starting-churches-from-scratch role **not where Christ has already been named** (verse 20) has been largely **accomplished** (15:18) in the eastern Mediterranean. Third, we see this unique phrase of Paul's, "the gospel of God," in 1:1 and 15:16.[14] And finally, Paul lays out in 1:10-13 his determination to visit them, why he's been prevented thus far from doing so, and his desire for their financial help (as we just saw in 15:22-32). So, we clearly have this special **wormhole-like** connection between early Chapter 1 and mid-to-latter Chapter 15—all about apostleship.

Clearly therefore apostleship in chapters 1 and 15 is a vital theme for the whole letter—as bookends. One could almost say that 1:16 - 15:14 is a theological parenthesis![15] So what are we to conclude from all this? Surely Paul's letter to the Romans is the most thorough and exquisite explanation of the gospel and our salvation in all of Scripture. But it is imperative for all believers to keep in mind that it is wrapped on both ends by what is also the clearest explanation of ministry of pioneering after Christ's ascension. The whole Church must never forget how the two go together. When he wrote **Romans**, providing a textbook of theology for seminary classes was not on his mind, but rather the necessity of world mission.

A Quick Summary

1. Contemporaneous with the Twelve—the big 'A' Apostles—were several others who are called apostles in the New Testament, i.e. small 'a' apostles. [And the first person so identified was Barnabas, not Paul.] The role of the Twelve was unique and non-repeatable, but their *going out* calling was not unique.
2. The core calling of all of these was and is to "go and make disciples of all nations" (Matthew 28:19), particularly "not where Christ has already been named" (Romans 15:20). Though we have not dealt with "church planting" per se, it is clear throughout the New Testament that the aim of these pioneering ministries was to see people won to Christ and become communities of faith and discipleship. To be a disciple in isolation from the Body is a contradiction.
3. Throughout history there have been many, many small 'a' apostles; and there still are.
4. The New Testament apostolic teams were comprised of apostles and "fellow-workers." The latter were not apostles, but no doubt had a variety of giftings; and their role and contribution were essential. When Paul said, "We have received...apostleship" (Romans 1:5), he almost surely was thinking of the many fellow workers as well. If you're a fellow worker and tempted to feel of lesser importance, realize that your name stands in heaven among such as these: Andronicus & Junias, Aquila & Priscilla,

Aristarchus, Artemas, Clement, Crescens, Demas, Epaphras, Epaphroditus, Erastus, Euodia, Jesus Justus, John Mark, Luke, Philip, Sosthenes, Syntyche, Titus, Trophimus, Tychicus, Urbanus, and Zenus!

Some Practical Considerations

XBB Apostles?

Of course, apostolic teams are not only westerners or expatriates coming into a country from the outside. Christ gives apostles to the church **to equip the saints for the work of ministry, for building up the body of Christ** (Ephesians 4:11-12). This is especially crucial in the early days when the gospel is beginning to penetrate a people for the first time, and then soon after as the churches begin to send out apostolic teams across the country and beyond. We've seen throughout history and even today how things really surge as the Lord raises up apostles and their fellow workers from among the indigenous people. These will be HBBs (Hindu-background believers), BBBs (Buddhist-background believers), MBBs (Muslim-background believers), TBBs (Taoist), JBB (Jewish), SBBs (Shinto)... You get the idea.

My friend Rory and his family used to live in a particularly very hard and unreached country. Then because of the war they and nearly all expats had to leave. Health, living conditions and safety remain atrocious for the many millions of citizens who can't leave. Recently Rory ran into Faisal, a church leader with clear apostolic gifts in his 50s from that country, who was briefly outside of it. Rory desperately plied him with many questions about how things were going. After a while Faisal said, "Rory, I can see that you are so burdened by our country and that you yearn to come back as soon as possible. We so very much appreciate your heart for us! However, the time of ministry for you expat workers is over, at least for now. God has used you to successfully get things started. But it's now our turn. We must take up the mantle for the spread of the gospel and apostolic work in our country. And God is doing it through us. The number of believers in fellowship has risen from 500 a few years ago to around 3,500 today."

Just parenthetically, Faisal also shared this story with Rory. He had been in prison five times because of his faith. Not long ago while in solitary, they put a 20-something man in his cell, and Faisal was grateful for the companionship. The other man said he was in for murder. At the mosque he was asked to kill a *kafir* (apostate). So, he went to the man's house and killed someone who fit the description, but it turned out to be the wrong guy. Eventually Faisal realized how he was the intended target. So, for the next couple of months he just loves and serves the man, with food, a pillow, and guidance on how to get by. Very sacrificially. Eventually Faisal tells him who he is, and the young man is stunned. But now he feels so grateful and loyal to Faisal there's no way he'd kill him. Faisal tells him to come visit after they both get out, and he'll help him with employment, etc. The guy does visit and comes to faith. As a side note to this side note, a mutual friend of mine and Rory's used to disciple Faisal years ago.

Can Apostolic Teams Reproduce?

Can they be catalysts in the formation of new apostolic teams? 110% yes. In my opinion the apex of Paul's ministry—at least that recorded in the New Testament—is his work in Ephesus. For some time, even during his 2nd Missionary Journey, Paul longed to go to Ephesus. For a church planter like Paul it was the prize, the plum. But at that time the Lord blocked him from going there and sent the team up to Philippi instead (Acts 16:6-12). Perhaps Paul wasn't ready, having not yet honed his skills among large Gentile populations.

But during his 3rd Missionary Journey the Lord opens up the door for him and the team to the great city of Ephesus for a stable and extremely fruitful two-year work. There he concentrates on training believers (Acts 19:8-9). And we observe from ministries like Epaphras' to his home tri-city area of Colossae, Laodicea and Hierapolis,[16] that Paul likely sent out several teams of pioneer church planting interns. And the result was that "all the residents of Asia heard the word of the Lord, both Jews and Greeks," (Acts 19:10) a population estimated to have been around 15 million people at the time.[17]

The point is, Paul's Ephesus-based ministry not only reached the area around Ephesus but seems to have been an apostolic team reproducing machine! And in that way this huge population heard the gospel; and for centuries some of these churches were the strongest in the Roman world.

Field Level Decisions

In a recent training with a case study, the class was asked whether the appointed team leader—who was now without teammates—and his family should persevere where they were or perhaps move on to join another team. They had been there for many, many years without seeing much fruit, and were struggling. Everyone agreed that the issue came down to a simple one: Is this person an apostle or not? If yes, then they should stay (and recruit); if not, then they should move on and come under another's leadership.

Apostolic teams in the New Testament had enormous latitude with regard to direction and strategy. It's so interesting, for example, to read of the processing that went on inside Paul's team in the 2nd Missionary Journey, as they meandered from southern to northern Asia (modern day Turkey), and were then directed by the Holy Spirit to go across the Aegean Sea to Philippi, resulting in the first church in Europe.[18] In today's world of instant communications, there might be a temptation for sending churches or organizations to be overly directive or controlling. I'm not saying there is no role for them in some of the parameters. But I am a believer that better decisions are generally made closest to the scene of action.

Who Among Us Is an Apostle?

As a field director responsible for many teams across the 10/40 Window, I used to really want to know this, as I felt it could help me help the teams. Sometimes I felt I could sort of tell when first meeting someone, by such things as their vision, their sense of perseverance, their entrepreneurial spirit, their effect on others, etc. In *A Vision of the Possible* I even presumed to write a section entitled "What are apostles like?" But over the years I found that I often got it wrong, and that later on it might be some introverts who began to appear more clearly as having apostolic gifting and fruit.

Wouldn't it be great if there was an apostleship test you could just buy at the drug store, sort of like a pregnancy test? Bottom-line: I've realized that it isn't crucial for us to know for sure, and we don't want to go around pinning apostle-badges to people's chests. Generally I'd say that if a person has a strong sense that they must get out to the frontlines of some unreached people group, to do whatever it takes to win people to Christ and to form resilient communities of His followers, and if they have seen God use them in the past to launch fruitful ministry, then they may very well be an apostle.

At the end of the day, the question remains fuzzy for most leaders and workers. In the thick of real opposition to his authority stirring up in the Corinthian church, Paul was keen on re-convincing the church that he was indeed an apostle, not just in general, but especially to them, since he was the one God used to bring them into being as a church. Ironically, in doing so, he acknowledges that there was no universal consensus on the matter: "Am I not an apostle?...If to others I am not an apostle, at least I am to you, for you are the seal of my apostleship in the Lord." We probably have to be content most of the time with fuzzy definitions.

Helping Apostles Among Us Mature

I've seen so many instances of a team leader who was an apostle (as it would eventually become evident), but who would lose many team members over relational or pastoral struggles. In some cases, the word **hemorrhage** comes to mind. These were apostles who didn't yet know how to get along with and to keep their fellow workers motivated. And here were fellow workers who found it impossible to put up with an assertive yet immature leader and to deal with their idiosyncrasies, and who soon felt **the leading of the Lord** to go somewhere else. I like to play a trick on candidates. I ask them, "Team A is led by an apostle. He's terrible at taking care of people, team pastoral care is non-existent, lots of rough edges, and team life is full of tension—but phenomenal things are happening ministry-wise. Team B is the opposite. The team leader is a great guy. Working with him is a delight. Team life is a slice of heaven. You feel cared for, and even developed as a worker. But year after year nothing is happening in the Work. Where's the **spark**? Which team would you prefer to be on?" Would you believe that around 90% of folks vote for Team A? Once a wise candidate spoke up, "Why are those the only two options? That's unacceptable!"

She was right. We have a sacred duty to mentor our young, rough-edged apostles—especially the *sons of thunder* types. They need us! Here are some practical ways mentors or overseers of team leaders can bless them:

- Help them grasp that not everyone is like them. What compels them and their clarity of vision is unique. They need to give grace to others who may not be as driven or as full of faith or energy. Appreciate the strengths others bring, and how those gifts will be needed in due course. Learn how to affirm and encourage others.
- Don't despise how people need pastoral care and shepherding. If you're not the one to provide this, find other ways that these needs can be met.
- Discern when your strong leadership is appropriate assertiveness and when it is over-control.
- Know that everyone is different. People are wired differently. Get used to it. "Accept one another" (Romans 15:7). What may be aggravating, or worse, today can later become a source of variety and strength.

Just a couple of other points here. Given how it's not unusual for emerging apostle-types to have rough edges, we hope and pray that their sending churches can support them by wisely navigating between patience and correction. They are God's workmanship, prepared for good works, and almost certainly will need a very strong grasp of the Word and ability to minister from it. On the other hand, it's also true that the ministry that the Lord has in store for them on the field may not necessitate a seminary degree.

Prayer

When you see a team and team leader that don't feel it's important to pray much, how does that make you feel? Let's be clear: What you are attempting for Christ is **impossible** humanly-speaking. As it's been said, "You can do more than pray, after you have prayed. But you can never do more than pray until you have prayed." We don't just go to the most spiritually-resistant peoples on earth, with real spiritual battle, and expect a movement to pop up just because we share the gospel a little, have nice tentmaking jobs, and follow the latest methodology. Unless God does what only God can do, it ain't gonna happen. All the New Testament apostles and teams knew that, which is why they prayed so much.

I'm a firm believer that every field worker needs to be part of at least a **weekly prayer meeting**. It could be specifically with their team, or just a random group of people eager to pray regularly for the work of the gospel and people's responses. Did you catch that? **WPM. Weekly**—at least. Could be more. Less than that isn't enough. **Prayer**. Not the 2-hour meeting that has 113 minutes of a late start, singing, sharing updates, Bible study (even), 20-minute break for coffee and Susie's brownies, strategizing and listening to a nice talk from the web...and then 7 minutes of actual prayer. All those other things can have their place and be in there a little; but the absolute focus and bulk of the time should be given to actually praying as a group. **Meeting**, i.e. being together in a time and place. Regular. Committed. Led. Scheduled. New Testament saints understood this.[19] **WPM**.

As John Piper has said, "If prayer seems to you like a diversion from productivity, remember God does more in five seconds than we can do in five hours."[20] We all realize these are true statements.

It's Not Just 'Possible' but is Happening!

None of the above is theoretical. It's been happening through the centuries, and it's happening all over the world today, by God's grace.

First, a simple example from our daughter in Morocco. "After going through a Creation-to-Christ series with a friend, we got to the point of Christ's death and resurrection. Every week she would go and retell the story to her husband (who always seemed to have a hard heart when the men on the team tried to share with him). One day after listening to the story account, she looked at me happily surprised and said, 'Jesus died for me. He didn't just die for you westerners, but for all people!' It was good news that illuminated her heart and her face. She then went on to say she must be baptized. Her husband had the same response, and soon the two were baptized in a bathtub in front of their young kids and our team.

"For 9 years we lived in Marchica...just loving Jesus and trying to follow him closely (though not always doing so in the highs and lows of life). We regularly prayed that the Lord would bless our neighbors and all the families of Marchica and work the soil of people's hearts. We now rejoice how some fruit beginning to bud and grow, and can count at least seven people in the growing movement in the country being from our little neighborhood! One is a man and his son, who also led another neighbor to the Lord. It thrills us to think of this little group forming that are based in Marchica now! One is now working with the team in outreach through social media and spends hours in the evening chatting online with many, sharing Christ.

Dick Brogden writes concerning the history of the gospel in Iran: "Missions work is not complicated; it's just hard. Someone has to do the difficult, unglamorous labor of rolling away the stones. We cannot look at the phenomenal movement of Iranians coming to Jesus today without consideration of Robert Bruce who in the 1860s wrote from Iran: 'I'm not reaping. I'm not sowing. I'm not even plowing. I'm just gathering rocks from the field.'"[21] By most estimates there are now at least one million Iranian Muslim-background believers in-country, and *the Iranian church is the fastest growing church in the world today.*

For the earth will be filled with the knowledge of the glory of the LORD as the waters cover the sea. Habakkuk 2:14

Some More Encouragements

First, a reality check. There is much, much work to be done. And even today, only a small percentage of cross-cultural missionaries serve among the unreached.[22] While there are tremendous movements among unreached people groups today, the percentage of Christ-followers in the world is not keeping up with population growth. Still, movement growth

APOSTLESHIP REVISITED   25

is steadily increasing. "With 20+ years of reproducing churches, the number of Church Planting Movements (CPMs) has multiplied from a mere handful in the 1990s to 707 as of January 2019, with more being reported each month. Each movement's advance has been won with great endurance and sacrifice."[23]

For the sake of security, I have to keep things a bit general, not citing all sources, and not sharing some sensitive things that would also be very encouraging. Also, a lot of this is likely outdated and surpassed by the time you are reading it, which is good.

- Saudi Arabia: Somewhere between 400 and 1,000 Saudi Christ-followers today. A Saudi Muslim taxi driver told a friend recently (with no animosity) that there are Christians in every Saudi family. No doubt a wild exaggeration. But we praise God that the notion in people's minds that following Jesus is possible and may be becoming normative for some.
- Perhaps 300 believers in Libya. That is a painfully small number out of a population of nearly 7 million, but nonetheless a start.
- According to the 24:14 Coalition folks, at least 750 large, mature *movements* in the world today, comprising around 29 million believers, mostly among UPGs/10/40 Window. To qualify as a movement there needs to be at least 4 generations in multiple streams, reproducing, and typically having at least 100 believer groups meeting. Some are even in the six figures.
- How many from Muslim backgrounds are following Jesus today around the world? Estimates vary widely, from 7 million to around 20 million. This is astounding compared with how things were not very long ago (see below).
- The civil war in Yemen has been a devastating human catastrophe, and we truly grieve for all the suffering and death. But one silver lining is that there are now around 3,500 Yemenis following Jesus. That's still quite small out of a population of nearly 30 million, but it's encouraging compared to almost zero believers not long ago. A friend of mine visited the Jiblah Hospital there in 1983 and met an older couple that was retiring

after some decades of faithful service. They said during that whole time they had seen maybe one Yemeni come to faith.
- 1,000+ believers in Morocco.
- Thousands of disciples among the Darfur (Sudan).
- At least 500,000 MBBs in Burkina Faso today. Again, to grasp how remarkable that is, realize that there were only a handful around 40 years ago.

Four Stages of the Progress of the Gospel

Finally, we're so excited about how the gospel has advanced all over the world, even just during our time personally on the field. Let's take an example from the Middle East—even though the same analysis and encouragement could be drawn from many strategic regions. Consider these 13 Arab Mideast countries: Egypt, Jordan, Israel/Palestine, Lebanon, Syria, Iraq, Bahrain, Kuwait, Oman, Qatar, Saudi Arabia, UAE, and Yemen. When we first went out to Egypt a long time ago in a galaxy, far, far...well, this galaxy...there were almost zero believers from Muslim background in any of these countries. Ones and twos. Super unreached. ALL 13 countries being in what I'll now describe as Stage One. How the gospel progresses among a people group block or a country can be noted in four stages.[24] Again, reckon these as country-by-country:

Stage One *Seed Sowing*

> BEGAN around 1900
> NUMBER OF BELIEVERS: 1s and 2s, if any
> DESCRIPTION: Little or no "fruit." Valiant labor over decades by persevering workers. We were advised in the Eighties to forget about church-planting (though we didn't!).
> MARTYRDOMS: A few expat missionaries

Stage Two *Church Planting*

> BEGAN around 1985
> NUMBER OF BELIEVERS: A handful to a couple dozen

DESCRIPTION: CP Begins. Small fellowships form (though often would go out of existence in a while). Slow growth.
MARTYRDOMS: A few more missionaries

Stage Three *Movements*

BEGAN around 2010
NUMBER OF BELIEVERS: hundreds or even thousands
DESCRIPTION: Emerging (small) movements. Growth mostly in DMM/CPM type ministries
MARTYRDOMS: increasing number of local MBBs

Stage Four *Break Out!*

BEGAN: Not yet. But maybe on the verge in a couple of countries
NUMBER OF BELIEVERS: in the tens of thousands
DESCRIPTION: THE TIPPING POINT! Believers boldly take the lead. It becomes very public. No longer possible to hide or ignore. Millennials and social media may play decisive roles.

Remember that not long ago all 13 countries were definitely in Stage One only. How about today?[25] My best appraisal is that it is:

- 1 in Stage One;
- 4 in Stage Two;
- 8 in Stage Three (and 2 or 3 could be in Stage Four before long).

This is as of this writing. I believe that by the time you are reading this, the harvest here will have progressed even further. So, what's all this got to do with apostleship? Only everything. The gospel has taken root and grown through the Lord sending and using apostolic teams doing pioneer apostolic ministry as described above. All glory to Him!

SPOILER ALERT: Want to know how it all ends? There is a certain and intrinsic relationship between all those efforts around the world by apostolic teams, hailing from so many different countries, and the date that our Lord returns to Earth:

And this gospel of the kingdom will be proclaimed throughout the whole world as a testimony to all nations, and then the end will come, [Jesus prophesying concerning the Last Days as he sat on the Mount of Olives with his disciples, viewing the Temple area a short distance across the Kidron Valley, three days before the crucifixion.] Matthew 24:14.

At the vanguard of "seeing effective CPM engagement in every unreached people and place by December 31, 2025," and to "work together to start kingdom movements in every unreached people and place in our generation" with sacrificial urgency is the *24:14 Coalition*. You have GOT to read their vision, their commitment to monitoring progress, and their description of the current state of the Harvest in "Appendix 1: Movements Around the World." Some highlights:

- If a movement is defined as four generations of disciples gathered in churches, with a minimum of 1,000 believers, then we currently know of 1,350 movements today. More than half of these are among Muslims.
- "We know of approximately 29.5 million former Muslims and 30.5 former Hindus in these movements."
- "The vast majority of these movement efforts are being catalyzed by workers from the Global South."

Brothers and sisters, rejoice over what God is doing! As Steve Smith says, "Some generation will finish the final lap. Why not us?"[26]

---

1. Brogden, Dick. *This Gospel: A Collection of Missions Sermons.* Live Dead, 2018.
2. Source withheld for security reasons.
3. Matthew 25:21, 23.
4. Excerpted from Sinclair, *A Vision of the Possible.*
5. Adam Grossman, in an email to a friend of mine.
6. The men and women who give us our translations spend their whole lives learning New Testament Greek, with all its nuances. It turns out that the context demands that this participle be translated as one of "attendant circumstance," and acting in the same way as the finite verb, i.e. itself a command in the sentence. Matthew 2:8 is a similar construction.

7. We recall the mutual understanding they had with Paul in Galatians 2:8-9 of him focusing on Gentiles, while they would concentrate their gospel proclamation on the Jews for a period of time—still then a very unreached people group.
8. McBirnie, William Steuart. *The Search for the Twelve Apostles.* Carol Stream, IL: Tyndale Momentum, 1973.
9. "The intangibles of urgency and grit" by Steve Smith, Chapter 34 in Parks, Stan & Coles, Dave. *24:14 - A Testimony to All Peoples: Kingdom Movements Around the World.* Spring, Texas, 2019.
10. Cahill, Thomas. *How the Irish Saved Civilization: The Untold Story of Ireland's Heroic Role From the Fall of Rome to the Rise of Medieval Europe.* Anchor, 1996.
11. Overheard? "Derek is a bit of a misfit. Let's encourage him toward our missions group." ☺
12. Source withheld for security reasons.
13. First implying it in Romans 1:13. And because the allusions to their financial help are so unmistakable in 15:24-29, some viewed the whole book of Romans as largely a support-raising letter!
14. Only elsewhere in Paul's second letter to the Thessalonians (three times).
15. In Romans 1:15 Paul says he is eager to "preach the gospel" to the church in Rome. This makes no sense if we take that to mean evangelizing the lost. No, rather Paul is preaching or expounding the gospel in these fourteen and a half chapters of Romans.
16. In the Lycus River valley, after having traveled along the Meander River—which is from where we get our English word "to meander." When Paul wrote his epistle to the Colossians and Laodiceans, he had not yet met these new churches, but states how Epaphras was ministering under his leadership.
17. Per various Roman census figures at the time, ranging from 9 million to 20 million.
18. Acts 15:40-16:40.
19. Hebrews 10:24-25.
20. Found posted at www.desiringgod.org and on various social media.
21. From his 2019 daily blog, October 29, https://www.livedead.org/2019/10/29/dealing-with-the-dead/.
22. "Are you in?" by Rick Wood, Chapter 2 in Parks & Coles, *24:14 – A Testimony.*
23. "24:14—The war that finally ends" by Stan Parks & Steve Smith, Chapter 28 in Parks & Coles, *24:14 - A Testimony.*
24. From a talk I enjoy giving entitled: "Four Stages of the Harvest in the Arab Middle East Among Muslims: A brief look at history, where we're currently at, and a look into the future."
25. Not including some large expat populations in some Gulf countries.
26. "The storyline of history—Finishing the last lap" by Steve Smith, Chapter 24 in Parks & Coles, *24:14 - A Testimony.*

2

THE CASE FOR COUNTING

Five reasons measuring ministry progress is biblical and essential[1]

"Knowing your purpose motivates your life. Purpose always produces passion. Nothing energizes like a clear purpose. On the other hand, passion dissipates when you lack a purpose. Just getting out of bed becomes a major chore. It is usually meaningless work, not overwork, that wears us down, saps our strength, and robs our joy."

—Rick Warren[2]

Some activities in ministry just feel right: praying, preaching, sharing the gospel, leading a Bible study.

When it comes to other pursuits, sometimes we're not quite sure. The measuring of ministry results is one such activity. It continues to spark confusion and disagreement. Is it biblical? Or is it carnal, worldly?

Detractors will point out that God cares about people, not numbers. A focus on counting can lead to pride and self-dependence. And what about David's great sin of ordering a census? We've all experienced how setting numerical goals or tallying up numbers in ministry can make it all feel a little business-y rather than like a work of the Spirit. It also feels out of sync with the nature of our ultimate aims, which are spiritual and internal, as we long to see lives transformed from the inside out. How do you measure that? Measurements deal with the visible and tangible, but it's the invisible that has greater significance. How can you put a yardstick up against faith, hope, and love?

All good points. But before you dismiss any attempts to measure ministry success, hear me out. Here are five reasons why I believe quantitative appraisal in ministry is both strategic and biblical.

1. There's a lot of counting in the Bible.

God is not anti-numbers. The Bible even has a book called "Numbers"! We find throughout the Old Testament the counting and measuring of all sorts of things: days of Creation, years of lives, censuses of tribes and troops, and exact specifications for the Tabernacle and temples. Some people might have an aversion to anything numerical, but God doesn't.

What about actually measuring God-given tasks? Just one example: in Exodus 35:4-9 God commands the people of Israel to make freewill donations of gold, silver, and valuable materials for the construction of the Tabernacle. Then in 38:24-31, we get a glimpse of the people's overwhelming response: a detailed tally of all the materials contributed. A vague report of, "Praise the Lord, he provided enough for the project," would not have been the same.

The New Testament is also full of measurements. The hairs of our heads are numbered! (Matthew 10:30). Jesus cites numbers in the parable of the talents (Matthew 25:14-30) and of the minas (Luke 19:11-27). In the first miraculous feeding, all four Gospels explicitly mention the number of people, loaves, fish, and leftover baskets. When Paul writes about the reality of the Resurrection, he records how Jesus appeared to more than 500 brothers at one time (1 Corinthians 15:6), not just "a whole bunch of guys."

In the book of Revelation John shows concern for the number of people saved (5:9-10 and 7:1-10). In Revelation 7:9 we're told that about "a great multitude that no one could number, from every nation, from all tribes and peoples and languages." The number of God's redeemed is impossible to count. It's as if he's saying, we'd like to somehow count them all, but the work of the harvest has simply been too successful!

2. David's sin involved more than counting.

Whenever the subject of measuring in ministry comes up, David's sin of the ordering of the census is mentioned. Wasn't that his terrible sin? What a perplexing story we find near the end of King David's life in 2 Samuel 24 (and its parallel account in 1 Chronicles 21). Whatever it was that David did, it resulted in God's judgment and the deaths of 70,000 men. It also resulted in the acquiring of the land the Temple was later built upon (and precisely where Abraham was spared from sacrificing Isaac). This is a wonderful lesson about how God can accomplish good things, despite his servants' sins.

Clearly, the counting of troops was not inherently sinful. In Numbers 1 the Lord directed Moses to count all the fighting men. And at the beginning of David's reign, all the troops available to him were evidently counted (1 Chronicles 12:23-37). So what was David's sin in this instance? Whatever it was, it was immediately clear to Joab, who strenuously objected, though he was overruled. And David himself was convicted of the offense in his conscience immediately after receiving the report, even before the judgment was pronounced through the prophet Gad.

Joab must have sensed that David was moving beyond a reliance on God to relying on human capacity and strength. There was pride. There was also probably ambition beyond the Lord's mandate, perhaps he was even contemplating **empire** in the ways of the near eastern despots. Some also note that 1 Chronicles 21:6 seems to imply that David was planning to deploy even the Levites into battle, which was a violation of the Law. Whatever it was, he was disregarding God's faithfulness and leading with a secular mentality. His heart was off track.

If this were the only story in the Bible about counting, then one might surmise that counting, per se, is problematic. But it is only one example of counting among dozens. It is the only negative case, whereas the others are all positive. There are cautions for us in David's sinful census. But dispensing with measuring God-given objectives is not the lesson to draw from this event.

3. Tracking the ministry's progress encourages the people closest to the work.

As we see in both the Old and New Testaments, there are multiple instances where people tracked the success of the missions they'd been given by God. That just makes sense. If something is worth doing—and what is more worth doing than the sacred commission given to us by Christ?—then it would make no sense not to care whether or not it's being achieved. That would mean we're careless and complacent. Only with measurement can we get a glimpse, however imperfect, of the progress toward attainment of a goal.

Counting is principally a tool for the benefit of those closest to fruit production. It helps them revise their strategy and tactics by aligning their efforts with what God is doing. It is a way of seeing. It is not primarily to send stats up to leadership, though that too has its place. As the workers see progress being made, they are encouraged and rejoice in working with God. Imagine: we are measuring the supernatural!

But what about actually **gauging** ministry progress, the number of people reached, that sort of thing? That's exactly what we find throughout the book of Acts (emphasis added):

- **1:15** In those days Peter stood up among the brothers (the company of persons was in all *about 120*)...
- **2:41** So those who received his word were baptized, and there were added that day *about three thousand souls*.
- **2:47** And the Lord *added to their number* day by day those who were being saved.
- **4:4** But many of those who had heard the word believed, and *the number of the men came to about five thousand*.

- **5:14** And more than ever believers were *added to the Lord, multitudes of both men and women,*
- **6:7** And the word of God continued to increase, and *the number of the disciples multiplied greatly* in Jerusalem, and a great *many of the priests* became obedient to the faith.
- **11:24** And a *great many people were added* to the Lord.
- **19:10** This continued for two years, so that *all the residents of Asia* heard the word of the Lord, both Jews and Greeks.[3]
- **21:19-20** After greeting them, he related one by one the things that God had done among the Gentiles through his ministry. And when they heard it, they glorified God. And they said to him, "You see, brother, how *many thousands* there are among the Jews of those who have believed."

4. Measurements don't have to be perfect to be useful.

Sometimes we're viewing what is happening with a few individuals or a family, and that is a good thing. Other times, however, we need to see the bigger picture, perhaps even reckoning hundreds or thousands or more. Of course, God cares deeply for each person and each family. But those are on His heart not more so than the wider collection of His children. We might struggle to hold the two views together—the **micro** and the **macro**—but there is no such tension with Him. We count and measure progress toward the bigger goals **because** He and we care about people.

Suppose ten people in an unreached environment come to faith and their lives are being transformed. That's a cause for rejoicing. What if later on the ministry is counted and 300 are saved? That sounds more like a statistic. But in reality, what it points to is 290 more individuals, and many whole families, touched by grace. And taking it further, if you're in an apostolic endeavor to reach an unreached people group or city, you're now that much closer to the wider group being reached than when there were just ten. It's not that one is about people and the other about numbers (and pride). Both are about people, and God's glory.

I've already mentioned the tension between the invisible (what's happening in people's hearts) and the visible (what we are normally able to count). The qualitative versus the quantitative. As we are in the business of heart-change, how do we go about this? As Albert Einstein is rumored to have said, "Not everything that can be counted counts, and not everything that counts can be counted." But this complexity is not a reason to give up on measurement. We oftentimes have to rely on what some call proxy measurements. For example, you want to see changed lives but perhaps all you can count are things like baptisms or how many people are participating in fellowship and serving. Those markers will not provide an infallible picture of spiritual life, yet they are good indicators of growth. Again, they are not perfect. Only God has complete knowledge of what's happening in people's hearts.

These tensions can be challenging for mission efforts in general and the newly planted churches. The church is both a family and an organization. It's **organic** (not so countable), and at the same time **structured** (more easily measurable). Most would agree that the more significant dimensions of Body life are the spiritual rather than the easily quantifiable. As a good friend of mine says, "Measuring the soft stuff is always a challenge, yet these measurements often reveal more about the true state of ministry than the hard numbers." Of the various "seekers" around, how are they doing in their journey to Christ? Are unbelievers attracted by the lives of believers? Are believers growing in their apprehension of God's love, and how is that affecting their lives? Are people in the fellowship groups really linking in relationships, or just coming to a meeting and leaving? Are struggling marriages or families overcoming and being healed, or falling apart? Do we have nice **programs** but are failing to make disciples? Are disciples truly advancing in character and overcoming harmful patterns, as they learn to lay hold of the Spirit's resources? Is there God-pleasing unity in the church or painful discord? Is the next generation (the youth) also moving in the right direction for the Kingdom?

The intangible areas are hugely important, and yet nearly impossible to measure. It's good to acknowledge this difficulty. And where we can measure, we remind ourselves that we track the visible primarily as a means to assess progress in the internal and spiritual.

Despite these hurdles, here are a few suggestions for gauging such intangibles:

- Track attendance at important meetings.[4]
- Follow the number of new professions of faith or baptisms each year. These proxy measurements indirectly show if members are motivated to share their faith and if unbelievers are being transformed by the gospel.
- How many who attend exploratory groups, such as Alpha, are embracing Christ and joining the church?
- Track how many members are meeting with other individuals for growth and mentoring.
- Track people moving into leadership roles for the first time.
- Have staff members report when they see members have personal breakthroughs, such as overcoming addiction, confessing disobedience, or taking bold steps of faith.
- Consider conducting an annual survey asking objective questions about subjective realities. For example, ask small group leaders, "On a scale of 1 to 10, how would you rate the relational health of your group?"

5. Measuring helps you lead more effectively.

We need to know if things are moving forward, or if we are just **busy**.

> The old definition [of field work] was an assorted mix of activities defined as mission. Like many organizations, [for example, a particular] agency had mainly measured activity (e.g. number of missionaries sent, kinds of ministries started, money donated, etc.) rather than results. In fact, some of the leaders felt that we should not try to measure results. They believed: 'We should just be faithful and leave the results to God'—despite the fact that the book of Acts often describes measured results.[5]

Ministry leaders have a sacred stewardship to give oversight, direction, and encouragement to fellow workers. And measurement gives insight into what's working and what isn't. An overseer needs to encourage those under his care. But how can you give affirmation to what you can't see?

I've had the privilege of serving as a field director in a mission agency. In such a role you regularly see encouraging things and encounter great stories. But you also see suffering, martyrdom, teams that break up, even immorality and marriages falling apart. But nothing causes me more joy than seeing how the Lord brings about a Harvest through our collective efforts, however inadequate and imperfect.

Measurement brings us closer to seeing things from God's perspective. If counting ever moves us toward pride or self-reliance, then we need to repent. The glory for anything positive must always and immediately go to Christ, and not to people or organizations. But if we're in prayer and operating in the Holy Spirit, then knowing where things are at should just make us all the more dependent on God.

Only the Father knows the precise progress toward the fulfillment of Jesus' promise in Matthew 24:14. But each of us engaged in making disciples and bringing this "gospel of the kingdom" to unreached people groups have a little piece of the harvest field to go after. Tracking and measuring how that is going in each of our respective spheres is not only a very helpful thing to do, it is the biblical thing to do as well.

---

1. This first appeared in *Christianity Today/Leadership Journal* online, 2015, except for some minor differences. Reused here with permission.
2. Warren, Rick. *The Purpose Driven Life: What on Earth Am I Here For?* Zondervan, 2012, p. 33.
3. As previously mentioned, this was around 15 million people at the time.
4. Hebrews 10:24-25, "And let us consider how to stir up one another to love and good works, not neglecting to meet together, as is the habit of some, but encouraging one another, and all the more as you see the Day drawing near."
5. "Moving an organization from routine mission to launching movements" by S. Kent Parks, Chapter 42 in Parks & Coles, 24:14 - A Testimony.

3

BAPTISM IN RESISTANT CULTURES

Time for a Change[1]

"It has gone from sitting in a chair and being washed with dippers of water (an Asian type of ritual), to a whole group, when they read over and over again about baptism, going to a river together, standing in the river in a circle holding hands, and on 1, 2, 3 going under together. In another group, they simply choose one of their salat washings to say, this day, this washing, is my baptism identifying with Christ—his death and resurrection."

— an account from Southeast Asia (see below)

I was recently conducting my two-day training on "Church Planting Essentials" in a North African country among workers from a variety of agencies. While we were discussing "How to disciple Muslim-background believers (MBBs)"[2] a brother raised his hand and asked, "So where does baptism fit in here?" Clearly from his Southern Baptist background, this was not something to be skipped over. I confess to having been a bit bothered at first, thinking this is complicated and it would get us off-track. But I proceeded to give my normal **song and dance** about how the whole area of baptism needs more examination and how most ministries to Muslims haven't yet sorted this one out. But even as I was speaking the thought arose in the back of my mind, "He's right. I'm tired of muddling and dodging this issue."

Most of the examples in this chapter are about **MBB**s. But they could just as easily be about HBBs, BBBs, JBBs, and so on (Hindu... Buddhist...Jewish...).

While there certainly has been some baptizing of believers in many of our ministries, so many other teams have shied away from baptism because it's too problematic. It's almost as if there's been an unspoken agreement among some of us: "Though we'd love to see the MBBs in our ministries get baptized, we understand if most of them don't want to. It's a problem waiting for a good solution." You know all those verses in the Bible indicating how baptism can be delayed indefinitely? Yeah, me neither.

It is the contention of this chapter that this is no longer good enough. We owe it to our dear brothers and sisters from various backgrounds to lead them toward obeying Jesus' command of baptism. But let me be quick to add: I am not advocating that we pressure them, or that we just get them to do it because we say so, after a token Bible study—nor that we, the expatriate church planters, necessarily do the baptizing. At the end of this chapter are some recommendations on ways to move forward.

Why Baptizing is a Problem

A year ago in a Levant country I was enjoying the rich hospitality of a brother, a "Muslim follower of Jesus." Because I knew that he was strong in his faith and testimony, that he was very knowledgeable of Islam, and that he hadn't yet been baptized, I asked him, "Are there any practices in Islam with water or washing that might be useful concerning baptism in Christ?" My intent was not to be provocative but simply arose from a desire to learn. But you would have thought my question was, "Are there clever ways for you to jump off this 5th floor balcony?" and he quickly changed the subject.

The first problem is that in most of our contexts baptism is viewed as a rite belonging distinctly to the Christian religion. If there is a Christian minority, it is of "them," not at all of "us." For a Muslim to be baptized is therefore perceived as a clear act of converting out of Islam and into Christianity: socially, culturally, and maybe even legally. And we're all aware of how it can also easily be perceived as a betrayal of one's family and cultural heritage. For those ministries in which new believers self-identify as "Christians," this isn't a problem. So be it. But for those aiming at a more contextual approach, not wishing to convey conversion[3] in a social and cultural sense, this is a genuine dilemma. The hope is that the perception by one's family of apostatizing[4] can be avoided. Please don't fail to read "The Story of Alma" (Appendix 7). Her grappling with issues of identity is very enlightening.

The second challenge is that of heightened persecution. Although the act of baptism in some resistant contexts isn't a big deal, in others it is perceived to be a huge, irreversible step, virtually inviting severe retaliation from the family or local population.

These are very real problems and issues. But should they leave us in a state of avoiding baptism in our ministries? Should the perplexities keep us in a stalemate, waiting in a sort of holding pattern for someone to figure out how to make it all easy? No. Despite the hurdles—which do indeed need to be addressed—we must move forward in baptizing for three compelling reasons.

1. Because Jesus Said So

The rite of baptism was developed during the Intertestamental Period and was famously utilized by John the Baptist. John's baptism centered on repentance and climaxed in the baptism of Christ himself (though ironically, he had nothing to repent of). Then after Jesus' resurrection and before His ascension he gave extraordinary training to the Eleven, *"appearing to them during forty days and speaking about the kingdom of God."* (Acts 1:2-3) Wouldn't you love to have been part of that! It was during this time that Jesus made it clear that from now on all His followers were to be baptized. However, this would not merely be a baptism of repentance, but one signifying full identity with Christ (in the Father, Son, and Holy Spirit). Cleansing from sin was also in view, but perhaps of lesser significance than our connecting as His disciples with

His death and resurrection.[5] Baptism was to be the experiential and visual sign of a complete life-change, as He is now my Savior and Lord.

It is in this context—as we saw in Chapter 1—that Jesus gave the simple job description of particular significance for all apostolic church planters: *"Therefore go and make disciples of all nations, baptizing them in the name of the Father and of the Son and of the Holy Spirit, and teaching them to obey everything I have commanded you"* (Matthew 28:19-20, NIV).[6]

In hindsight, I realize that for years our teams were guilty of a kind of **obedience-optional** way of discipling. In the back of my mind was the notion that the risks and consequences my dear Arab MBB friends face are different and more severe than my own. So, I must not press them too hard. But such discipleship is actually a contradiction. A disciple who doesn't want to obey Jesus is not a disciple. We all struggle at different times with different pressures, but the authentic intent of the heart of a real follower is to submit to and obey Him. This is why I love the emphases of **Disciple-Making Movements** (DMM) methodology, which we will explore in Chapter 4. From the very beginning, the core of this approach is that people learn what God says in His Word and determine how to obey it. Each week in a "Discovery Bible Study" (DBS) the participants read and reflect on a passage of Scripture. Even for pre-believers, the key question becomes, "If this is God's word, then how am I going to obey it?" The answers must be in the form, "I will...." Once the group become believers, the question simply changes to, "Since this is God's word, how am I going to obey it?" It is so encouraging to learn that across the 10/40 Window in DMM-type ministries new believers are being baptized in larger and larger numbers. As indicated earlier, this is true in ministries among Buddhists, Hindus, Shintoists, Muslims, and many other societies.

2. The Crystal Clear Teaching in Acts and the Epistles

In the New Testament there are 106 occurrences of **baptism** (plus **baptize**, **baptist**), 44 of which are in Acts and the epistles. In the book of Acts, we find nine instances of people being baptized:

1. Pentecost: 2:38, 41;
2. Philip in Samaria: 8:12-16;
3. Ethiopian eunuch: 8:36-38;
4. Paul: 9:18; 22:16;
5. Cornelius and his large group: 10:47-48;
6. Lydia and her household (in Philippi): 16:15;
7. Jailer and his family (in Philippi): 16:33;
8. Corinthian believers: 18:8; 1 Cor.1:14-16;
9. Ephesian disciples (formerly John's): 19:3-5.[7]

Most of the references in the epistles (5 of Paul, 1 of Peter) refer to their experience in actual baptism and then draw a spiritual inference from that.

Most or possibly all instances occur immediately upon faith, though we can't always be sure of the time between believing and being baptized. But in no place do we see a substantial gap of time.

There does not appear to be any difference in the practice between different apostles. Some have suggested that baptism as such was a particular Jewish rite of initiation. While that may have been true of John's baptism, it clearly became applicable to Gentiles in an ongoing way. No variation can be discerned between the baptism of Jews and Gentiles, or of the practice varying between one cultural context to another. Indeed, Ephesians 4:5 ("*one Lord, one faith, one baptism*") stresses the singular nature of baptism for all believers, and this was written to a predominantly Gentile church. In no context was it considered optional.

Surely many of the Gentiles baptized in the book of Acts would not have been familiar with baptism, as such, beforehand. Just as many of our believers today need explanation and persuasion, so it was with believers centuries ago.

3. The Power of the Definitive Step

We know that spiritually, in the inner person, coming into the kingdom of God changes everything. That is why we are given so many terms for this metamorphosis: we're **born again**, we **move from death to life**, we're **a new creation, the old has gone, the new has come, we have a new citizenship**, we've **died with Christ** and **been raised with Him**, we're now **seated with Christ in the heavenlies**, and so on. How sad then if we rob our brothers and sisters of the privilege of reinforcing this new life in the dramatic and never-to-be-forgotten act of baptism! In their faith, they have crossed an eternal threshold. And the Bible clearly teaches that they should symbolically cross the threshold through water. Imagine the sad results in a person's heart over the years if this never happens. Ambiguity in one's life can be deadening.

Likewise, if somehow, however unintentionally, we convey to them that partial obedience is OK and that remaining an unbaptized *closet* believer is OK, is that really OK? Then we're somehow shocked when the church doesn't form and progress. Yes, the fears and dangers they face are significant. If I was in their shoes, I doubt I would do better in terms of conquering such fears. But can we trust the Holy Spirit to work in their hearts and give them spiritual power to overcome? I believe we must.

Bounded Set vs. Centered Set?

If you have already read much about "Bounded Sets vs Centered Sets," you may be tempted to skip this section. But please stay with me here. It has become vogue lately to say that a person from an unreached or resistant people group coming to saving faith in Christ is a **process**. It may take a long time. We can never know when he or she "crosses the line" to faith. Indeed, is there a line? If there is, what is it? And is it my job, really, to know who is "in" and who is "out"? Therefore, we shouldn't press people toward decisions or definitive steps, but rather just keep pointing our friends to Jesus.

Almost always the bounded versus centered sets theme is cited. You know, bounded sets mean that those who are "saved" or "in the church" or "going to heaven" are those who are on the right side of a line, usually a line of profession (or baptism) or theological understanding. Some favoring a centered-set approach say no, that that is too artificial and a poor reflection of what's invisibly happening inside the heart. What truly matters is whether one is moving **toward** Jesus rather than **away from**

Jesus, regardless of what side of the line they're on.[8] That is, does their arrow point toward the Center or away from it (Him)? For example, in **bounded set theory** during Jesus' ministry Judas would have been considered "IN," whereas Nicodemus would have been "OUT," which is not really how things turned out, was it? So I understand this. I get it.

However, I believe these concerns and arguments are, at best, half-truths. They take a few biblical points, but completely ignore many dozens of New Testament passages. The simple fact is, in the book of Acts and in the epistles, it was extremely clear who was "IN" and who was, well, not yet in. This is utterly true in the book of Revelation as well. It was also a significant theme in Jesus' teaching. It's just that in the Gospels the form of His followers see-sawed from small to large to small to medium, people coming and going—His **group** always being a bit amorphous. Jesus knew this is how it would have to be until the Church would be solidified and established at Pentecost. At that point, clear identity in Christ became very important.

When one enters the Kingdom of God through faith in Christ as Lord and Savior, she is entering into the New Covenant which Christ inaugurated. Jesus emphasized this, especially in the Upper Room. With covenants, you're either in or not in.[9]

I have to admit I'm not wild about the word "saved." Sounds very much "old-time religion," doesn't it? But we find it 163 times in the New Testament (**salvation, savior, save**), and "saved" is the terminology so often used to denote being right with God, of being a true believer/follower/disciple of Christ.[10] Less frequently used phrases include being "obedient to the faith" or "entering the Kingdom of God." It is abundantly clear in the various passages that there are those who are presently "saved" and those who are not, or a time when an individual was not saved and then he is. Was there a line that one crossed? Absolutely. While it is beyond the scope of this book, I'm convinced from the extensive and consistent New Testament data that the experience of saving faith—of crossing the line, if you will—is a combination of what must happen internally and externally. On the inside, we read many times that we must repent and believe. And we also read that on the outside, in our actions, we must confess our faith, be baptized, and get involved with Christ's *ekklesia* in community. What happens in the heart is salvific and the outward actions are essential visible follow-through steps. Does this mean that what is visible (e.g. being baptized or part of a believers' group) is always 100% true of spiritual reality? Of course not. But the exceptions to that would have been true in the early church as well,[11] and it's not something that put the apostles off.

Bottom-line? All the fuzziness factors, the issues of nuance, and our inability to peer into the human heart do not diminish the need for us to teach disciples to obey all that Jesus commanded, including baptism.

So Where Do We Go from Here?

I'll be honest with you. In my role in the Middle East when I pondered our teams moving ahead with the aim of baptism among Arab MBBs, I would kind of **gulp** and wrestle with a sense of unbelief. I'm nevertheless convinced it's the right thing to do, that we must operate in obedience, and we must trust God to provide for His expanding church.

DMM teaches that a major transition point in successful DBS groups is that the seekers become believers. Really, at some point in successful groups people begin to fall in love with Jesus. They confess faith in Him. At that time then, for a season, some DBS passages can be about baptism. Of course there will be resistance. Even lost people often have a genuine respect for baptism. But the believers are then soaked with God's Word concerning this vital step. Certainly, the expatriate church planter does not pressure the new believers to get baptized. Indeed—as we'll see—he or she is probably not even in the meetings. But as the pattern has already been set for the participants studying the Word and deciding how they will obey the particular passage and subject, so it is with baptism. At some point people say, "Yes," from their hearts. What is the role of the expatriate church planter in this? It is a vital one, as he or she gives leadership from the outside, coaching and training the **person of peace/group facilitator**, establishing direction, and setting passages to study.

In most contexts, the prospect of baptism will raise the issues of contextualization and identity. Are these new ones in Christ now "Christians?" Or are they "Buddhist/Muslim/Hindu **followers of Jesus**?" Something else? They will likely make these determinations for themselves, and they will figure out how it shapes for them the step of baptism. These are good discussions to have. About the issue of baptism being seen as culturally Christian, it should be stressed with the new believers who are studying it that baptism pre-dates both Christianity and Islam, and it has never been a symbol of a changed religion, but rather of a changed heart.

I'm not personally aware of anything that would suggest that baptism must be public. However, it does seem normative for it to be with other believers, as one thing it does signify is becoming part of the community of faith. And it serves to be an edifying, faith-building community experience, reasserting and rehearsing the truth of the gospel every time a believer is symbolically crucified, buried, and resurrected with Christ.

While I'm an immersion guy personally, I believe we need to be flexible regarding the form of baptism. The new churches will likely be deciding this question for themselves. It won't be for us to say, "Hold on. You must get every square millimeter of your body underwater for at least three seconds in a bathtub, lake, or church baptismal."

I'd like to close now with an account from a very "high-identity, high-practice" context in an Arab country. The story below is not unique, as we are hearing of more and more MBBs being baptized, in good numbers, even in the **trickiest** of places. This encouraged my heart, and I trust it will yours as well.

> Dear friends... Bob & I were driving back today from a 2-day prayer conference when we received an SMS from our dear MBB "Matt":
>
> "hi bros, all is fine. pray 4 the guys... SAI [a key mosque leader] is guided by the Holy Spirit(*) 2 b baptized 2moro at 9am... Joe & SAA [a new MBB who'd been studying the Word for 2yrs in the group!] were encouraged and they will get baptized too. "Ian" will join us too. Pls pray for such an advanced step... more Lord Isa!"

We & others have been praying for this to happen for months, and when we got the SMS we almost jumped for joy were it not that we were driving in the car (!!) :-)

This is BIG. this is the 1st MBB imam that we know of who is getting bptizd, and not just one, but TWO on the same day!!! They will be bptzed in [certain body of water]. And our fellow brother in the Lord "Joe" who rejoined the flock about 6 months ago will also be baptzd. These significant steps of obedience, in line with JC's commands and the Word's exhortation are, we sense, a tremendous leap forward for the Kingdom here. At our conference, it was prophesied that BIG things will happen in our region in 2012. It's already beginning...

Obedience is growing.

Praise God.

Tobias

(*) The Spirit-led stirring behind this all is that SAI had a vision from the Lord about 7-10 days ago - while he was praying, he saw (while his eyes were open) himself coming under a waterfall and being washed by this powerful fountain!! As soon as he saw this he knew in his heart the Lord was speaking to him about being bptzd! (He had witnessed Ian's bptsm last year on the beach... and knew that Matt had been baptized 5yrs ago.) so after spending several days studying the Word about this with the other brothers in their study grps, he knew his time had come :-)) --- isn't God good!?!?[12]

---

1. Except for some minor differences, this chapter first appeared as, Sinclair, Daniel. "Baptism in Muslim Ministry: Time for a Change," in Mission Frontiers, May-June 2015, *Transform World*. Available at https://www.missionfrontiers.org/issue/article/baptism-in-muslim-ministry. Reused here with permission.
2. The term "background" does not necessarily mean something in one's past and not one's present. I believe that the term "MBB" can broadly refer both to those who consider themselves former Muslims as well as those who self-identify as Muslim followers of Jesus.
3. Except for proselytes to Judaism, none of the occurrences of "convert" (both noun and verb) in main English translations refer to conversion in an outer, social identity sense, i.e. the way it is normally *heard* today.

4. Arabic *kafara*.
5. See Grudem, Wayne. *Systematic Theology, An Introduction to Biblical Doctrine*. Leicester, UK: Intervarsity Press, 1994. Ch. 49.
6. Note from verse 16 that this was a command specifically to the Eleven apostles. While this *great commission* probably has general application to the Church, its particular application is to those called to apostleship.
7. This was their second baptism. Clearly baptism in Christ was markedly different from John's baptism of repentance.
8. Paul Hiebert's original paper on "bounded-set thinking" did indeed encourage differentiation "between those who are followers of Jesus and those who are not," even with a centered-set view. But many since then have taken these new approaches to disparage the importance of such. Paul Hiebert's personal lecture notes on "Set Theory and Conversion," along with further references, can be accessed here: http://hiebertglobalcenter.org/blog/wp-content/uploads/2013/04/Lecture-Note-36-Set-Theory-and-Conversion.pdf.
9. Two of the three references Jesus makes to the "church" are about church discipline. That, of course, pertains to boundary points (along with issues of personal restoration).
10. This includes a range of past or aorist tense, present tense (usually in the passive participle), and future tense (i.e. *will be saved*).
11. E.g. Simon the Magician's baptism in Acts 8.
12. Source withheld for security reasons.

4

DMM FOR DUMMIES

"You can count the seeds in an apple, but you can't count the apples in a seed. When you teach, you never know how many lives you will influence...you are teaching for eternity."

— Karen Jensen[1]

"So one seed from one apple has now produced some 2,250,000 MORE SEEDS."[2]

Of course you've heard of *"XYZ" for Dummies* books. I'm not saying any of you are actually 'dummies.' But this chapter seeks to boil down the principles and personal discipline necessary for church planting in the Muslim world so that everyone can easily understand and apply them.

I am not an expert on **Disciple-Making Movements** (DMM). In fact, it's rather the opposite. If I am considered an authority or expert by some, by contrast it would be in the area we might term **traditional church planting** (CP). You could say that the content of *A Vision of the Possible*, which first came out in 2005, was **pre-movement** stuff. It was not about seeing lots of small fellowship groups come into existence and multiply exponentially. Instead it was about how a team in a resistant environment works to see one church formed, and then hopefully grow and multiply, i.e. what some call "0 to 1." There was discussion of movements in it, but it was fairly vague, and that might have been a reflection of the mission community's lack of clarity on it at the time. Also, beginning in the late 90s many mission organizations and the Vision 5:9 Consortium began to use a tool called the "(Seven) Pioneer Church Planting Phases."[3] By Version 3.0 it contained something about movements, but was more of an emphasis than a methodology. Like my first book, the CP Phases have been viewed more as pre-movement and traditional "CP" in approach.

As I was introduced to DMM, I quickly became convinced, and it was with the zeal of a convert—a big paradigm-shift for me. Several years ago, as field director for our Middle East region, I was speaking to all our region's workers and shared some frustration. We rejoiced that the overall number of Phase 5 and 6 fellowship groups of Muslim-background believers (MBBs) was growing—which meant 3 or more believers regularly meeting together—but many were disintegrating almost as fast as new ones were starting. Three steps forward and two back. Very few were solidly growing in maturity and size, becoming more resilient and viable, and seeing MBB elders raised up. I also expressed, as non-judgmentally as I could, my view that a key reason for this was that most of our dear brothers and sisters were hiding and only obeying Jesus' commandments quite selectively. Of course, I quickly clarified that if I were in their shoes, I would be doing worse.

Not long after that I met with a leader from another agency in Jordan who shared with me that they had launched out in DMM and were seeing hundreds or even possibly thousands of believers, with rapid growth. (Sadly this movement also had its disintegration moment shortly thereafter. It is one of the 18 movements researchers record that have disintegrated out of a current 1,350 movements being tracked.) Anyway, sometime after that I had my first weeklong DMM training and was filled with hope that there just might exist solutions to how traditional CP was holding us back. In particular I was struck how five particular emphases from Day One could be integrated well into church planting:

1. Working with a group, not just individuals;
2. Having seekers and believers in the Word;
3. Emphasizing obeying Jesus;
4. Creating the expectation that group members share each week what they are learning with at least one person outside the group (which implies some overcoming of fears);
5. Mobilizing the apostolic team to engage in much strategic prayer —which so many teams were not doing.

Around 2007, as more of our teams began to go down these tracks, we were seeing lots of ministry growth in our region: 210 fellowship groups across Jordan, Lebanon, Northern Iraq and Syria. It's more now—that was years ago. The Lord had taken these ministries to a whole new level of boldness and fruitfulness, and nearly all the increase was in **movement-oriented** ministries. Whole families were following Christ. New believers were **asking** to be baptized. A few were willing to face any risk or cost in order to openly proclaim Christ—and some paid those huge costs. By the grace of God, a new day had dawned. To get a glimpse of how the Lord of the Harvest is using movement ministries around the world, I would again urge the reading of "Appendix 1, Movements around the World."

A Quick Definition or Two

A very important clarification is needed here: By "DMM" I am not promoting a particular methodology. A friend of mine counted 14 different approaches to **church planting movements** or **disciple making movements**, not to mention how some teams do a "hybrid," combining different parts from varying approaches. I think that's great. Variety and experimentation can only help in the long run. My aims with this chapter are to promote **movement thinking** and **movement practice**, and to give an introduction to how you can get started.

Though there are some slight differences between the terms, 'CPM' and 'DMM', most people use them almost interchangeably. Virtually all mission agencies working among the unreached today are taking a close look at church planting movement methodologies. Over 90% of our own community's teams in the Middle East have adopted movement practice fully or partially. The number of Muslim-background believer groups in this region has tripled in the past four years, and nearly all that growth has occurred in DMM ministries. We will examine the 16 vital elements of movement methodologies and compare and contrast these with more traditional approaches. But how can one define a **church planting movement**, or a **disciple making movement**? Here are three helpful definitions

David Garrison: "A rapid multiplication of indigenous churches planting churches that sweeps through a people group or populations segment."[4]

Stan Parks and Dave Coles: "A Church Planting Movement (CPM) can be defined as the multiplication of disciples making disciples and leaders developing leaders. This results in indigenous churches planting churches. These churches begin to spread quickly through a people group or population segment."[5]

Jerry Trousdale:

> In recent years, we have concluded that "disciple making" is a more accurate term than "church planting" to describe the core biblical principles at work in these rapidly multiplying movements...In a nutshell, Disciple Making Movements spread the gospel by making disciples who learn to obey the Word of God and quickly make other disciples, who then repeat the process. This results in many new churches being planted, frequently in regions that were previously very hostile to Christianity. All the principles that we are seeing at work are clearly outlined—indeed, commanded—in the pages of Scripture.[6]

I won't attempt to improve upon these, but I will just point out the following:

• In whatever we call it, should we emphasize **church-planting** or **disciple-making**? I believe in church-planting through and through. And I believe it is very present in the New Testament. But, as a friend of mine says, if you go after church-planting, you might get disciples. If you go after making disciples, you will definitely get churches. So I'm presently leaning toward emphasizing disciple-making. Nonetheless, they are two wings of the same airplane. In this chapter I'll generally refer to DMMs, just to keep things consistent. Also please be aware that there are other specific methods out there with other names that still more or less belong in the CPM/DMM family.[7]

- The hope is that, by the power of the Holy Spirit, the outcomes are multiplication and not merely addition—and steady multiplication growth is exponential. [Having said that, a big **shout out** to those who heroically labored and saw some **addition** in previous generations!]

- DMM is meant to be applicable to super resistant or unreached populations as well as responsive ones. One can find many examples around the world of both.

- DMM has been called a **method** or **methodology** or **strategy**. Though we might bristle at that because it sounds a little programmatic, I think we have to become comfortable with it. I have never heard anyone teach that if a team just does A, B and C steps, then churches are guaranteed, perhaps as the ministries of John and Charles Wesley and George Whitefield—i.e. Methodism—were understood in the 18th century. Bottom-line: it is an **approach** to doing things (with a lot of variation around the world) that aims to be biblical and relies 100% on God for seeing results. We focus on making disciples, and God establishes His churches.

Who is This Chapter For?

My aim in this chapter is to lay out some biblical principles to persuade the reader on a few points, and to provide a few skills. The latter will be very meager, since that's difficult to accomplish through a book. Indeed, this brief chapter will not give you all you need to launch out well into DMM. Around the world there are often 2-day introductory trainings, followed by peer-to-peer mentoring, and these will provide a better foundation. Also, reading the books on this topic by Trousdale, Parks and Coles, and Garrison would be helpful.

If you are untrained in DMM, this will be a good introduction for you, as you are at the early part of the **hockey stick** (see Figure 2 below). If you have received training, it will serve to remind and reinforce DMM concepts. And even if you are well-experienced in DMM, hopefully this brief writing will be useful to remind you of DMM principles and practices, and perhaps serve to point out aspects that might have gotten overlooked in your work along the way. A friend of mine does tons of training in all levels of DMM, and coaches some large DMM ministries in northeast Africa. He says he always finds it valuable to teach or review the basics because it causes him to "recalibrate."

You, as Trainer

Before beginning to unpack DMM, let me mention something parenthetical but potentially vital. It might be that the Lord will use you not so much to start a new movement, but to train others who will launch movements. These might be special believers from the dominant group (e.g. Muslim-background believers), Christian background believers of the ethnic group (CBBs), or even expats. Here are a couple of brief examples from a colleague:

One time I invited an MBB to an event. But no one knew. They were all Christian background and just assumed the same of everyone else. Anyhow, during the training there was skepticism with people saying it couldn't work. But a lot of the objections were really just "Muslims would never do anything of this." So they were blaming the harvest instead of the workers. My friend was staying quiet, but internally getting frustrated. He saw people full of doubt and disbelief and also blaming the harvest. Finally, after Day 2, he stood up and questioned the doubt and disbelief and said we should stop saying that, "They won't do this." Because he thinks they will do it, and he knows, because he is one of them. Then he said, to show them he was going to go start his first group. Then he left. People didn't know what to say. The next day he came back and indeed had started his first discovery group the night before.

Another story is of a local CBB I trained and then had him co-train with me a few times, and now he is training others. He has traveled to one country where they have had trouble getting groups started. He started training some local believers, and in a year and a half they have 4 generations—easily over 100 total groups so far. "Things are growing so fast they are out of control."[8]

It is indeed a new day. And we stand on the shoulders of those who labored before us, with whatever method!

So What Is a Movement Approach?

The Seven CP Phases—which were popular in the 90s and 00s—kind of went like this:

- Phases 1+2 Forming the team, landing and getting settled on the field, learning the language pretty well;
- Phase 3 Evangelism;
- Phase 4 Discipling those who respond to Christ;
- Phase 5 Forming believers into a fellowship group, 3 or more. They might already know each other, or they might not;
- Phase 6 This fellowship grows in number and maturity toward a *critical mass*, and at the end of Phase 6 elders are appointed;
- Phase 7 More growth, maturing, and hopefully multiplication.

It was similar to, and borrowed from David Hesselgrave's "The Pauline Cycle,"[9] and made perfect sense. Of course, it was understood that this was not a rigid set of steps but rather a general sequence, and there could be much overlap. For example, when our team was in our first year in Alexandria, Egypt we had a fellowship group of MBBs, even though we were all in the early stages of learning Arabic.

So dear reader, let me ask you a question: Based on what you know so far about movement approaches, with which method would you say it is easier or harder to achieve the first fellowship group of believers (aka "0 to 1"): the CP Phases approach (aka traditional) or DMM?

Some people don't like lists. Others live by lists and have lists of lists. I'm kind of a list person, but the older I get the more tedious they seem. Anyway, since this is just a thumbnail introduction, I have to give you some lists here to introduce you to DMM. We don't have room for lots of stories here. The other books I just mentioned above contain loads of inspirational and encouraging movement stories, which will help these lists come alive for you. I'll also point out that these lists are meant to display general **defaults** that those involved in movements live by. They are not a silver bullet, nor are they hard and fast rules. Rather, they are beginning points meant to encourage deeper exploration and adaptation as the Lord leads.

16 Vital Elements of DMM

If one could distill the various aspects of DMM into one brief collection of priorities, it might be something like these sixteen, grouped under the subheadings of: In General, Early Stages, Early **Discovery Bible Study** (DBS) Meetings, and Advanced Stages.

In General

1. Loads of prayer. We are counting on God to do a miracle or two to get things started. As John Piper exhorts, "Prayer causes things to happen that wouldn't happen if you didn't pray."[10]

2. The aim is reproductive, exponential growth. Simple 'addition' will not be enough. **Discipleship Groups** starting new groups is always the aim, and not mere one-on-one discipling. "The general guideline is: 'Could an average young believer start and organize such a church?' Otherwise, church planting will be left to a few highly trained individuals."[11]

3. The outside (apostolic) worker leads strategically: meeting with the facilitator of the DBS before and after each session, setting the course of lessons, and shaping movement structure. The worker usually does not attend the DBS sessions—though there are exceptions—as the goal is for the local to be the people-gatherer and ultimately the facilitator.[12]

4. DBS meetings will always include a simple Bible study. This is not a 'taught' study, but rather an inductive study that all in the group participate in discovery.

5. Obedience to God's Word is emphasized from the beginning, generally by each person answering the question each week, "If or since this is

God's Word, this is what I will do in response."

Early Stages

6. Abundant sowing by the team, with a wide variety of people.[13]

7. Aiming to have a local, who will gather a group to do DBS. Many call this person a "person of peace" (POP), a la Luke 10:6 (see below). They will lead or facilitate this group, not the worker. Such a person is not necessarily a believer, or mature, or even a leader-type. But they will have a measure of confidence or influence. (Think woman at the well, Lydia, Philippian jailer, Cornelius.)

8. If it takes a long time to find a person of peace, that is OK.

Early DBS(s)

9. The DBS will go through a specific set of lessons or stories in the hope that all or most of the group will decide to become believers in Jesus and the Gospel.[14]

10. Besides the Bible study components, meetings also include sharing, praying for each other, worship, accountability of what's been done to obey previous studies, and possibly some service in the community.

11. Along the way, now and in future stages, members of the DBS are urged to share what they are learning each week with at least one person outside the group.

12. The *DNA* of reproduction is emphasized from the beginning. When this **seeker group** becomes a **believer group**, each member is urged to form their own DBS group with lost people, often continuing on in the original group.[15]

Advanced Stages

13. DBS groups go through lesson sets according to their stage: seekers (to become believers), early believers (to learn to be disciples), disciples (to become a church) or more advanced (e.g. leadership development, multiplication).

14. As the number of groups grows, it is important that everyone learns how this approach toward a movement works, down to the lowest generation.

15. Likewise, information about groups periodically moves up from the lowest generation to the top leaders.

16. At some point, groups want to move beyond just being isolated DBSs to also enjoying wider and healthier life of the church (*ekklesia*). Clusters of 4 to 8 groups are often the means for this. This also allows for recognition and empowering of gifts to a wider body (e.g. elders).

Comparison and Contrast

There you go! Simple, right? Don't worry if your head is spinning. To attempt a bit of clarity, let's compare and contrast traditional church planting and DMM. Imagine two teams going out to the field: Team A plans to do traditional CP, while Team B is committed to a DMM approach. How do those early stages look and where do they begin to diverge?

Take a good look at Figure 1. Try not to get hung up on the word "stage." I don't mean it as anything formal here (though they do correspond to the **Seven Phases** for Team A). I'm just trying to contrast the two diverging approaches.

STAGE 1: Pre-field prep will look pretty similar for the two teams, though pre-field training may not be exactly the same.

STAGE 2: Again, likely pretty similar, investing heavily in Language Learning.

STAGE 3: Similar but different. All in both teams are meeting lots of people, cultivating relationships, and looking for ways to engage people in spiritual matters. But here's the big difference: Team A folk are sharing the gospel and wanting to "lead people to Christ." Team B members may be doing kind of the same at times, but their objective, prayer and focus is to find a person of peace, someone God will use to launch a DBS, even if that person is not yet a Christ-follower. Let's call him Ahmad.

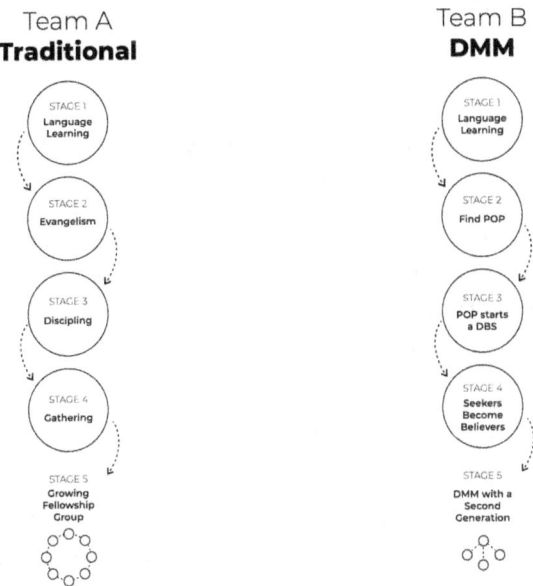

Figure 1 - Comparison of stages of CP and DMM

STAGE 4: Here things become very different. Ahmad is keen to learn more about the New Testament but isn't sure yet what to make of it for himself. His friend Mike (from Team B), encourages Ahmad that the best way to learn more about Christ is for him to pull together some of his friends to learn together. Mike calms Ahmad's unease with the commitment that, though he won't go to the meetings, he will meet with him every week beforehand to help him get ready. Ahmad gulps and agrees to give it a go. To his surprise, three of his friends say "Sure, sounds interesting." A simple **Discovery Bible Study** begins, as the group goes through passages provided by Mike.

Team A is working with a few individual believers one-on-one, helping them grow, and hoping they'll be open to meeting soon with other believers.

STAGE 5: Team A is able to pull together four local believers, two of whom team members led to faith and are from the same family, and two more that others on the team 'found.'

In the nascent DMM of Team B, the four of them decide that indeed Jesus is the way, the truth and the life, and together decide to become Christ-followers.

STAGE 6: Team A's fellowship group grows a bit. Now six believers. Two of the team members are very involved in leading and teaching.

Meanwhile, over at Team B, three of the believers eventually decide that they too would like to launch their own groups and succeed at pulling in some friends or family members. The DNA of multiplication is now firmly embedded. Team B now has quite a few leaders able to reproduce groups instead of depending on outside leaders.

Back to our earlier question: Which is easier? Here I can speak from experience. In the traditional CP approach, I've been directly involved and leading 3 different teams with Muslims to get to Phases 5 or 6 (believer groups), one even having around 25 believers in an Arab context. It seems almost funny now since numbers have grown a lot since, but that was one of the largest ministries among Arab Muslims in the Middle East and North Africa at the time. DMM-wise, I've been involved as a coach and overseer for a handful of teams whose ministries became quite large, as well as many still at what is Stage 3 above. In my limited experience, for a team working cross-culturally from scratch, it was easier or quicker to get to Phase/Stage 5 (gathering/group forming) in the traditional approach than it can be for a DMM team to get to Stage 5 above (having a regularly meeting DBS of believers). So why do I advocate DMM? Because our goal is not just a small, fragile group of believers here and there, which may disintegrate—as was often the case with traditional approaches. The goal is a movement where thousands (at least) will follow Christ. As we've seen around the world in the past couple of decades, a movements approach has the best likelihood of seeing that happen.

The bottom-line is that DMM may take longer in the early days ("from 0 to 1"), but then have much more potential to really take off with exponential growth. That's where the **hockey stick** analogy comes in. See Figure 2. A hockey stick has a long handle, around 4-5 feet long, and a blade to strike the puck which is around 10 inches long. It may very well take longer for things to get going well (the long handle). But when they do, the increase can be dramatic (the nearly 90° turn upwards). The reason it may take longer is the miracle required to find that "man or woman of peace" among the local population who is so interested in Jesus that he or she is willing to start and lead a Discovery Bible Study with some trusted friends or family, and all the social risk that implies. Such is the needle in the haystack. See Persons of Peace below.

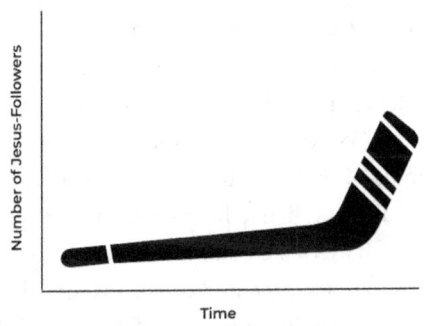

Figure 2 - Hockey stick depiction of growth in DMM

Normally things take off when the early believers get a big vision for their wider people or tribe. **Only obedience-oriented disciples change the world.** A friend in the Middle East shared with me this poignant example:

Omar came to faith and I immediately stressed the importance of reaching into his own community with the good news. He agreed in theory but it didn't seem to me like much was happening. I tried different ways to encourage this but it didn't seem to go anywhere. One day we were doing a study together and he stopped midway and started to stare off to the side. He had tears in his eyes and slowly said 'I wish my dad could have known.' It was such God moment.

Right away God began to multiply Omar's faith among family and neighbors.

And consider this from East Africa:

> I was approached by about 10 people who wanted to follow Jesus as they were disappointed with their former faith because their people group was suffering ethnic cleansing by the Arab majority in this country.
>
> They had no idea what it meant to follow Jesus but they just wanted a change. They asked me if I could rent a room for them so that they could have church and meet there. I was excited about their interest but answered to them: "I really would love to help your understanding of who Jesus is, but I cannot rent a room for you." They said: "We only need a small room, not expensive at all, please help us." I then told them that I could not help them with that, but that I would like to help them to become people who will be able to share this Good News to their whole tribe. They were surprised that they could do that as they didn't know anything at all themselves, but it did raise faith in their lives. We agreed to meet twice or three times a week to come together for three months and then they would go back and share this with their friends and families. During the training period they started two small fellowships and then they went and practiced what they have learned. Most of them are continuing doing what they have learned and at least one of them is part of leading a growing emerging movement among their people group.
>
> The lesson is: Speak faith into seekers or believers not just to get saved but to be used as an instrument to share the GOOD NEWS to their families and friends and people group.[16]

All apostolic teams, DMM ones included, will likely see various attempts not work out. A group will get started, and then flop, and people disappear into the woodwork. Scott Hamilton,[17] Olympic gold-medalist in figure skating and brother in Christ, said this: "I calculated once how many times I fell during my skating career — 41,600 times. But here's the funny thing: I got up 41,600 times. That's the muscle you have to build in your psyche — the one that reminds you to just get up."[18] DMM and apostleship call for that kind of perseverance.

Which is More Biblical: Traditional CP or DMM?

I'm convinced that both are perfectly biblical. While I used to be attracted to the traditional approach, in how it seemed to perhaps more closely mirror Paul's very active role within the church plant at Ephesus and other places, I began to get over that. I found these features to be particularly compelling in a movements approach:

1. The emphasis on the Kingdom of God (and NOT on "Christianity" or becoming Christians, in a social conversion sense). We find the phrase **Kingdom of God** 142 times in the New Testament, the word **Christian** only 3 times, and **Christianity** 0 times. And in none of those instances are people urged to "become a Christian." Rather, it's a call for people to become disciples.
2. The emphasis on learning from the Word from the beginning, with believers and even seekers having to grapple with it and apply it.
3. The emphasis on abundant prayer.
4. The emphasis on obedience for all disciples. I think this is where our community failed in earlier times, and why the groups were so fragile.
5. Finding "bridge persons" or Persons of Peace. (See "Persons of Peace" below)
6. Members of the DBSs sharing what they're learning with others outside the group. A friend of mine that was helping to spearhead a movement among Muslims in the Levant years ago —that was seeing hundreds of groups—told me that all are asked 2 questions each week during the DBS: 1) What are you going to do to obey what we learned today; and 2) Who are you going to share it with?
7. Not allowing fear to control the groups.
8. Using brief "*shema* conversations" (see below) in evangelism, instead of feeling that the interaction wasn't worthwhile if you

didn't go in-depth. We'll discuss what these are more later. Suffice it to say here that they are brief **hooks** to share spiritual ideas with many, to see who are the special ones God is already readying in their hearts. We find Jesus and others using this approach often. Some, however, will prefer to go for fuller explanations, for example the popular "Creation to Christ"[19] or "Kingdom Circles"[20] presentations.

9. Reproduction and multiplication. Exponential growth is all throughout Scripture and in the natural world. It's God's way. Consider: God brings about billions of every species and plant, from the simple start of Genesis 1. Israel grows from 12 sons to 2 million in a short period of time (Genesis 12:2; 22:17). We see the same principles in the sower's good soil increasing a hundredfold (Matthew 13:8). And in the parables of the mustard seed and leaven (Matthew 13:31-33). In the millions who heard the gospel in Paul's Ephesus-based ministry (already mentioned from Acts 19:10). And in the Church that grows from 120 persons in Acts 1:15 to many billion: "A great multitude that no one could number, from every nation, from all tribes and peoples and languages, standing before the throne and before the Lamb" (Revelation 7:9). Simple **addition** is not God's preferred method.

Any Objections?

Before we wrap this up, let's touch on a few objections that some people have with a movements strategy. While I—and this chapter—are pro-DMM, I don't wish to imply that the approach is a magic bullet or a cure-all for your CP problems. That would not reflect reality nor be fair to the reader. Here are some issues that sometimes give people pause:

- Getting from 0 to 1 (going from no believers to having one or more groups of regularly-meeting believers) can take a long time. We've already dealt with this. It's true. But once you get to '1,' the table is better set for multiplication.
- "Where is biblical body-life or *ekklesia* in a DBS group? Won't

such a format keep believers shallow in their understanding and faith?" I also struggled with this for a long time. To this complaint I counter: How about driving to an auditorium once a week, hearing a lecture, singing a song or two, then going home? Is that a recipe for depth? In even a single DBS, believers are meaningfully engaged in each other's lives and grappling with real issues. And every movement that becomes sizeable that I have learned of, there evolve clusters of groups, larger gatherings at times, the raising up of elders and teachers and people learning to operate in their gifts, and the sending out of evangelists and apostles to other peoples and places. None of this is automatic. But it is possible and does occur. Just as a mini-case study, I've had the privilege of getting to know a remarkably gifted Afghan brother, 'Farouk.' For security sake, we won't mention which ethnic group or city. He and his wife came to faith many years ago, and when much persecution broke out in 2010, he wound up spending a month in prison. But the Lord used that in Farouk's heart, and he came out with a burden for his people and a robust vision for movements. With almost "no effort" they saw 60 come to faith, and various individuals started Bible studies. Now there are 600-700 believers active in groups, four generations and over 20 leaders in three different networks. The Lord is using people with a variety of gifts, and they have been able to upgrade the quality of the studies through standardized lessons sets. Lately the persecution has resulted in *increased* unity among the networks, even if they're from very different backgrounds.

- "Rapidity leads to immaturity." Again, compared to what? The slow and steady approach in the west isn't doing really great. Here I would direct the reader to Don Dent's treatment on this question, *Decisive Discipleship: Why Rapid Discipleship Is Preferable and How It Is Possible*.[21] In movements the focus is not on "rapid," it is on "immediate." Immediate obedience and sharing is the goal to "make disciples" and "teach them to obey"—a result of that is often rapid growth.
- "Movements work fine in easy countries like Ethiopia, Burkina

Faso, India and Indonesia, but what about in difficult, persecution-heavy Islamic or Hindu environments?" First of all, many of the movements we have seen in Africa and Asia have been exactly in such difficult environments. North India was called "the graveyard of missions," but that didn't stop a wonderful movement from breaking out among the Bhojpuri.[22] In fact, these large movements seem to occur *more* in high persecution areas. As mentioned in Chapter 1, of the 77 million people in church planting movements worldwide, there are approximately 29.5 million former Muslims and 30.5 million former Hindus (see Appendix 1). And even among peoples where there is as yet very little fruit—such as where we are presently laboring—I believe the movements approach has the best potential for seeing indigenous faith and growth. No method brings a guarantee. But a reproduction-oriented strategy is the best way for us to get the sails up for when the Holy Spirit begins to blow.[23]

Persons of Peace

If you've been anywhere near CPM/DMM discussions, you will have heard of "POPs." This idea comes from Jesus' sending out of the Twelve recorded in Matthew 10:5-15; Mark 6:7-13; and Luke 9:1-6; and also from his subsequent sending of the 72, recorded only in Luke 10:1-12. The tag is derived from Luke 10:5-6: "Whatever house you enter, first say, 'Peace be to this house!' And if a **son of peace** is there, your peace will rest upon him. But if not, it will return to you." Then these teams of two each would heal the sick and share the good news of the Kingdom—not to mention "raise the dead, cleanse lepers, cast out demons" (Matthew 10:8). The son of peace designation is not found in the sending of the 12, but there we do find the idea of going to a town, asking which is the worthy family that hosts strangers, and hopefully staying with them. That family could become the conduit for the message. See Appendix 3 to view these passages in parallel.

To our modern ears, this sounds terribly presumptuous, especially since Jesus also states you'll be getting all your meals from them, and not ordering from Uber Eats. Reality is, however, that this was the dominant hospitality practice among Jews and Arabs for centuries. I remember a Jordanian professor telling us that this is exactly how things worked in the city of Salt, Jordan as late as the 1950s. No hotels. Travelers would just hang out at the town square, and before nightfall one of the good families would take them in. It was an honor thing. So Luke 9 and 10 are actually not strange in the historical context (and also reflected in Job 31:31-32).

Some teachers of DMM say that these passages show us how we are supposed to be conducting pioneering ministry today. It's a prescription, a methodology, a template, and that many apostolic efforts fail because they don't follow it. Others would say it's not a prescription but a pattern. Here's the idea:

- The gospel workers arrive in an unreached city, and strive to bond well with the language, culture and people.
- From early on they pray for God to lead them to a POP—a man or woman with whom they connect particularly well, who is especially interested in Christ or the Scriptures, with potential to influence others. Normally God has been working on this person's heart in advance.
- That man or woman, this POP—whether believing yet or not—gathers some family, friends or work colleagues to investigate further matters of the gospel. The prayerful hope is that this person would facilitate a study group, under the guidance of the apostolic worker.

So, do you think that the sending of the 12 and the sending of the 72, and the son of peace motif is prescriptive? That it is normative for pioneering work?

EXERCISE: Think of all the reasons pro and con to answer this question for yourself. Compare notes with others.

Here's my take on it: I see those two sendings as special. On these unique occasions Jesus instructed the disciples to go out to the villages only with the bare essentials. But I have never seen a missionary family travel to their destination without extra clothes, tablets for the kids, footwear, cash, credit and ATM cards, and then stay with a local family for weeks without remuneration. **Nonetheless, insights and patterns from these sendings are helpful, I will still use the POP designation, because it is useful.** Teams often talk about PPOPs too, i.e. Potential POPs.

However, there are definitely lessons we can derive from these sendings that we can adjust to our modern contexts. What we also consistently find in the gospels and the book of Acts is God uniquely using bridge people, individuals who are impacted and then who become gateways for the gospel to many others of their people.

EXERCISE: Cover up (quickly!) what is immediately below. And think of as many examples in the Bible of "bridge people" as you can think of. Compare notes with others.

Here are 3 classic examples:

- The Samaritan woman at the well (John 4..). I love how this is portrayed in the drama *The Chosen*.[24]
- Cornelius (Acts 10). Peter's first foray among Gentiles.
- Lydia (Acts 16). Her little group became the catalyst not only for the city of Philippi, but that church was the first church in Europe!

Here are a few others, and there are more:

- Government official whose son was sick (John 4).
- Gerasene demoniac (Mark 5).
- Ethiopian eunuch (Acts 8).
- Philippian jailer (Acts 16).
- Jason (Acts 17).
- Noble Bereans (Acts 17).
- Jewish leaders of Rome (Acts 28).

Finally, here is something remarkable, both in Scripture and in contemporary practice. Don't think that the POP has to be the most respected, educated, influential, spiritually-minded person you encounter. Sometimes it's quite the opposite. For every noble, respected Cornelius, there is an outcast woman at the well. We recall that she was considered a person of no importance. Zero, or less than. But in God's plan she became pivotal in starting the movement of Samaritans into the Kingdom. We often simply do not know who God is going to use powerfully. I have heard that in one movement in Africa, the most prolific POP and launcher of many successful DBSs was a 13-year-old girl. Experts also report that there is no standard personality type.

This story is not atypical of how the Lord works to prepare persons of peace:

> "Today is my birthday," noted Miriam, my refugee friend who recently came to faith in Christ. "This morning, I was looking at pictures of my birthday party from last year when we were still in Syria. With my fancy dress and my gold jewelry and invited guests—I thought I had it all. Then we fled the war and I lost everything. But it just occurred to me that I am so much happier today, because now I have Jesus!"
>
> Miriam is an inspirational young Kurdish woman from Syria who is married with two small children. Along with her family, she barely escaped the fighting last year and moved to our host country in the Middle East. They were desperate at first and our church provided some basic needs. But then she began attending worship services with her husband and father. Something about the music, Bible teaching, and the love they felt from Christians gripped her heart.
>
> Since Miriam was raised in a strict Muslim context—praying five times a day and having memorized the entire Qur'an—starting to follow Jesus was a big risk at first. But today she's facilitating Discovery Bible Studies to other Kurdish women with passion and insight. She and her husband are telling everyone about their new faith in Jesus, despite the persecution they face.[25]

Jerry Trousdale says it well: "People of peace are God's pre-positioned agents to bridge the gospel to their family, their friends, or their workplace."[26]

DMM Counterintuitives

In DMM circles one hears a lot about **counterintuitives**—in other words principles or practices that at first seem off, backwards or maybe even unbiblical. So trainers often have to urge new people to Hold On. Don't bail out on this. Wait till you've got the fuller context before making value judgements. Here are 13 such counterintuitives that a list-ophile will appreciate:

- **Go slow to go fast.** Be diligent but patient in the early days when it seems no progress is being made. Praying, searching for God's POPs, and planting seeds IS progress.
- **Our role is vital, but not being in the middle of the group(s).** If you read the chapter "The Role of the Church Planters in Church Planting" in *A Vision of the Possible*,[27] then you'll understand how I struggled with this one. From my experience with a handful of MBB fellowship groups, it seemed problematic to depend on just one local leader in the group to stay aware of what was happening. It's like you're viewing the group through a straw. But then I witnessed a mini-movement in Jordan, and how the groups were able to multiply quickly, partially because it was 100% indigenous from the beginning. And as things grew, the expat *stand-alongsiders* were able to develop relationships with a few other leaders in the movement.
- **Disciple to commitment (not convert then disciple).** The old way: *evangelize* a person until they believe and confess the main bits (salvation through Christ and the cross, substitutionary atonement, deity of Christ and His Lordship, baptism, and pre-Tribulation pre-Millennialism—OK, maybe not the last one) and pray the prayer at the back of the booklet. Then shift gears and you can now *disciple* them and hopefully get them into a group with others (whether they know the others

or not). Quite clearly, that is not the way Jesus worked with people. He took them where they were at, as long as they were reasonably responsive to what they had. Over time they got more teaching, saw Him work, and experienced challenges to their faith. In such a context they all GREW. And His concentration with His disciples was not doctrine, but rather obedience and overcoming fear.

- **DBSs can be led by pre-believers.** In fact, this might even make it less threatening at first for Maryam to ask her friends to join her in pondering things.
- **Be spiritually conspicuous.** In the "old" days we shared Christ, but we also felt we had to be really careful. Otherwise we'll be pegged as missionaries and expelled. However, the more secretive you are, the more likely you will fail. Become widely known as someone with a vibrant relationship with God, and those He is working on inside their hearts will come find you out.
- **Focus on ordinary people, over the rich and powerful.** Again, isn't this what Jesus did? Would you rather work with a taxi driver who loves Jesus and eager to follow Him come what may? Or a high government official who is willing to study with you individually, but only secretly? Only one of these will multiply!
- **Concentrate your training on ordinary people, not vocational Christians.** Likewise paying local leaders kills growth. [Down the road as the network has grown a lot, a few going into half-time or full-time ministry with financial enabling may be appropriate.]
- **Focus on Families!** Not just individuals.
- **The DBS facilitator is just a facilitator.** Your POP friend is to get things going and weekly gently give guidance to catalyze discussion, sharing and group discovery. If they are the strong, natural leader type, and insist on teaching, that will put a hole in this life raft, and it is certainly not reproducible. Be aware, however, that this is almost always counter-cultural, as more Eastern cultures prefer and defer to the *strong natural*

leader. Not to discourage you, but some practitioners say this was the biggest hurdle to get over at the beginning, helping early Discovery group facilitators grasp the process.

- **Share only when and where people are ready to hear.** Don't feel that you must *unload the truck* (of your gospel presentation) on whoever you can get to listen. See **Evangelism below.**
- **It's about discovering and obeying.** It's not about teaching and knowledge. Don't tell people what to believe and do but help them discover it for themselves.
- **Focus mainly on a few very responsive people to win many.** Lots of seed-sowing or media follow-up can definitely help things get started. But ultimately loads of personal evangelism, or even mass evangelism, isn't going to bring the gospel to the millions.
- **Prayer is a super-high priority.** After all, finding that POP who will start a group, seeing it get going, and the group embracing Christ after some Bible studies, is a big miracle. Not to mention the burden of centuries of contrary thinking and spiritual warfare in the culture. We call on God's Spirit to accomplish the dramatic work in people's hearts.

Some DMM Myths

Myth #1: "There is no teaching in DMM." It was a paradigm shift when we heard from David Watson, a prolific trainer with Cityteam International, that the apostolic worker plays an extremely important leadership role from the beginning as he or she coaches the POP.[28] DMM is NOT a fire-and-forget picture of just finding the POP and letting things go. We are not merely vague catalysts and cheerleaders. This helped me personally drop my objections over Counterintuitive #2 above about our important but off-to-the-side role. We are selecting the passages from Scripture that the group will study (see Appendix 5, DBS Lesson Sets). And we might continue in an in-depth mentoring role with one or more group leaders. Those involved in 3+-generation movements report that they end up spending hundreds of hours in training and ministering the Word with multiple leaders.

Myth #2: "Language is not needed. Simply find a national POP who knows English—or use a translator—and she will figure out how to communicate to her people." No. Watson was stunned when he once heard back that some were getting this impression. While newbies on the field can be praying and sharing Christ briefly with friends, they need to concentrate on learning the language. It's those with a good foundation in the language and culture who are equipped to go all out in DMM.

Myth #3: "DMM is quick. Simply find your POP, introduce the DBS process, and turn 'er loose. Spend a lot of time in prayer and everything will work itself out." In some field contexts, things can begin to happen in a relatively short time. I've definitely seen that in some people's ministries. And in other contexts, people might labor faithfully for 10 years or more, with much prayer and seed-sowing, before this occurs. These are things beyond our control, but in the hands of the Lord of the Harvest. And is prayer the "main thing"? Not really. As mentioned, abundant prayer is indeed so very important (individually, in small groups, with partners back home). But to say it is **the main thing** contradicts the fact that God has us in place for a reason, to be engaged with the people.

Myth #4: "DMM has too much focus on obedience and it is legalism." All heresies are distortions of a truth. Legalism is the heresy of the truth which is obedience. More on this at the end.

Myth #5: "DMM is a guaranteed process—do the right steps and add water and a movement will surely sprout." Only God determines the times and places of movements! Again, the sailboat analogy is helpful here. Only the wind of the Spirit can start a movement. If our sails are up, in terms of prayer and using biblical patterns of multiplication, we can be used to help start a movement. If our sails are down, with human tradition and non-reproducible patterns, the wind of the Spirit will pass us by.

Evangelism in DMM

People assume that missionaries—or whatever word you prefer—share Christ with people a lot. Indeed *evangelism* is a very biblical concept, particularly in New Testament Greek. We have *euangelion* (the gospel or good news), *euangelistēs* (evangelist), *euangelizō* (to preach or evangelize; the middle participle can mean evangelism), and *kērygma* (proclamation or evangelism). And it is certainly associated with apostolic ministry. But would you be surprised to know that most field workers do not feel particularly confident in this area? A friend of mine goes all over the world to give training in evangelism to gospel workers. He will always ask the group this question: "How many of you feel like you have the gift of evangelism? In other words, you love to share Christ with people—whatever it takes to get into conversations—and you have seen God use you in this way to bring people to faith? Raise your hands." He says that quite consistently it's around 1 out of 5 that raise their hands.

So what about the 80% of missionary workers who don't raise their hands? Are they chopped liver? Are they defeated before they even start? Do their supporters even know this about them? (Yikes!) Can introverts do OK? Should the 80% go home? The answer, of course, is, "No." There are a variety of other forms of apostolic ministry that are required: discipling, teaching, leading, hospitality, strategic prayer, mentoring, mercy ministry, healing, logistics, and more. And all can use the gifts they do have **evangelistically**. On the bell curve of being weak or strong in evangelism, I'm on the left side tail of being weak—though I have a great appreciation for it. My wife is on the right-side tail of being very gifted and adept. I've noticed that when Liz strikes up a conversation with a local woman, it readily moves into life and spiritual issues. The other person is obviously wanting the dialogue to continue. For me, when I somehow get into a conversation over spiritual things, it sometimes feels like they're looking for the exit ramp. Can you relate? Anyway, Liz and I average out OK. Here is some good news about sharing the good news for the ungifted: **DMM takes off some of the pressure**.

All of us should want to sow abundantly—as abundantly as our other responsibilities will allow. Don't you want beautiful feet? (Isaiah 52:7)

All of us can tell God each morning that we are available to engage with people, if he will so lead us. We can look for ways to mention something in our spiritual life, even if clumsily, and for those who express illness or needs, we can ask if we can pray for them. Gifted or not gifted we can do these things. But if we're not especially skillful at it, that's OK. What do I mean?

Remember Stage 3 in the contrasting between Traditional CP and DMM in Figure 1 above? In Traditional CP you are keen to share as much of the gospel as possible with as many people as possible and lead them to make a faith decision. However, in DMM the primary aim is to find a Person of Peace, someone the Lord has prepared to be keen to learn more and to become a bridge person to others. So just a probing or brief mention of spiritual reality may suffice. Pressure off. See what God will do.

What is a "*shema*" statement?

The word *shema* comes from Deuteronomy 6:4, "Hear, O Israel: The LORD our God, the LORD is one." It's the Hebrew word for 'hear' (like the modern Arabic *sema*ʿ). In other words, what story, or illustration, or question, or brief testimony about the Lord in our lives—any of these can be quite brief—might prick the ears of our friend to hear more about the supremacy of Yahweh God, and the Savior He sent into the world? Could even a short unveiling by you of your walk with God lead them to confide what they have been thinking? You could think of these as a brief tester, or hook, or just something interesting and provocative. I've given many examples in Appendix 4, but here are just a few examples:

- They ask what you do or why you live where you do. This is perhaps THE most common question foreigners are asked. You reply with an answer to points to Christ's honor or calling.
- "This morning I was reading in the Bible and God showed me..."
- You ask, "In your religious upbringing, what did they teach about the Messiah?"
- "Thank you for sharing with me about your current struggle. That must be hard. Can I pray for you?"—maybe in Jesus' name.
- "Have you ever had a dream you think came from God?" So

many have seen "a man in white" in their dreams. It is then good to read Matthew 17:2 and/or Revelation 1:12-16 with them and ask if that is who they saw.

The conversation may not go much further, or it might open up. Or you might learn of the impact only later on.

In what contexts can you do this? Any. It might be with longtime local friends. With other family members as you hang out at their house or wedding. Or with someone you just met while getting your car fixed. Or by intentionally going out with a partner to coffee shops. Whatever.

Putting all this together

So is the *shema* approach THE way of evangelism in DMM? No, not necessarily. But it's a good approach. Nonetheless the whole gamut of ways to engage in spiritual conversations are still used across the board, depending on people's preferences and opportunities. Here are some examples you might want to try:

- Prepare a gospel presentation. An example is *Creation to Christ*.
- Prepare a personal testimony. This can be about how you came to faith, or how God worked in your family in an amazing way.
- Share Scripture. I love to ask my friend if I can read to them a few words of Jesus and have my Arabic Bible ready. Then I briefly read and comment, without sermonizing, on John 14:6 (The Messiah is very special), John 10:10 (He wants to give you a better life), and Matthew 11:28-30 (He can train us to change our lives. Maybe include v27 about Him revealing God to us.) My prayer is that they will want to read further on their own. Or that they will at least be troubled.
- Ask probing questions.
- Quote something interesting and **leading** from their holy book. "What does this mean?"
- Engage in an apologetical question, e.g. how we know the Bible is reliable. There are some great short videos on this in various languages, made by MBBs.
- Pray for healing for them or family members.

- Tell a funny story. A friend in Saudi Arabia loves to use stories about Juha, who is like an Arab Mr. Bean.
- Follow up contacts from social media campaigns.
- Show a video about something on your phone (or WhatsApp it to them). These days there are loads of really good videos out there (testimonies, apologetics, dramatized Scripture portions, etc.).

So try *shemas*. But if you prefer some other approach, don't let me stop you. We all can do *kērygma*, whether or not we are gifted. Whatever we do, we pray for God to open up those doors of encounters, relationships, witness and fruit. We especially ask the Lord to lead us to POPs.

What a Simple DBS Looks Like

Remember, the initial aim is to help a DBS group get off the ground, led by a local whom you are guiding. You personally might have DBS-type Bible studies with individuals along the way. But that is not an end-point. The purpose of those would simply be to show them how it can be done, and that it is not hard.

Please keep your finger here and also turn to Appendix 5, "A Typical DBS Meeting." As you can see, there's the start-up time before the Bible study, the Bible study itself, and some discussion after the study. In the Start Up, people are reconnecting and reviewing things from the previous week. The Facilitator is seeing how his friends are doing.

Normally the Bible study or story is over a passage—whether from the Old Testament or New Testament—one that is not too long or complicated. Later on they might take on longer or more involved passages, or do a topical study. During READ and Questions 3 and 4, the group is grappling with what they observe and what it may mean. Question 5 then is each person answering this: "What am I going to do to put what I have learned here into practice?"

And then the Closing time is so very important:

Q6: "How can we help each other this week?"

Q7: "Who will I tell what I am learning about God this week?" This refers to at least one person outside the group.

As the guide says, this is perhaps the most important question of the DBS time. Some even say, "If there is no Q7, then there is no DMM."

The Proposal

How could you possibly ever persuade your local friend to get two or more friends or family members to look into Jesus and the meaning of the Bible? The answer is, you can't. The Holy Spirit must do a work in his or her heart. But you have probably already had some good conversations together, and you have detected a keen interest, not to mention how they truly value their relationship with you. This might take the form of an eagerness to learn whatever they can, or a dissonance with what they have been brought up to believe, or some specific personal pain the Lord is allowing into their life. In any case, there's a receptivity, and you and your fellow workers are praying regularly for her.

You now feel the time is right to propose that she launch a DBS. What do you say? How do you approach it? Here's how it might go between you (Anne) and your friend (Latifa):

ANNE: Latifa, we've known each other for a while now, and I really value our friendship. I so enjoy our times together. And when we've talked about God and us and heaven, I see you have a tender heart for Him.

> LATIFA: Yes, I see it that way, too. You mean a lot to me and I thank God for bringing you into my life.
> ANNE: We have done a Discovery Bible Study (or learned a story) a couple of times. What do you think of that way to approach the holy books?
> LATIFA: I like it because it is simple. I always learn something new. I never saw Jesus in this light before.
> ANNE: I want to ask you about something serious. Can I do that? I think you could invite Maryam and Sheikha to study with you, to learn together about these things. What do you think?

LATIFA: I don't think so. That would be too hard. You know a lot more than I do. So I think I could ask them, but you should come and lead it.

ANNE: I understand what you are saying. But believe me, in the long run, it would be better if you facilitate the times, and I not be there. However, don't worry. I can come once or twice, if you want. After that I will meet with you before every meeting to prepare you, but I won't attend the group meeting. We will meet afterwards too, to discuss how it went. And, I will select what you guys can study, so you don't have to invent anything. Remember, you don't need to 'teach,' but only guide a discussion.

LATIFA: Well...(gulp) maybe.

ANNE: Great. Please ask God if He will help you do this. And let's see tomorrow how you are feeling. I will pray for you tonight. OK?

Simple, right? Not long ago, I was leading a two-day basic training, and before the end of Day One we all got into pairs and practiced **the challenge**. I could feel the confidence level of the group rise. The next morning one of the sisters was excited and wouldn't let us start before she shared what had happened. That evening she visited her local friend and challenged her to start a DBS, and she agreed! It was going to start the next week.

Please see Appendix 6 for some sample Lesson Sets. Typically the first group of studies guide a group of seekers to embrace Christ as Savior and Lord, to become believers. The next set helps them to learn what it means to truly be His followers or disciples. And the set after that teaches them how to be the church. Somewhere in there they are also encouraged to launch their own DBS groups. Soon, leadership development is also explored.

How to Be a Disciple

Disciple Making Movements are about making disciples. Funny that. Let's remember what that means. Do you remember what we said earlier was Jesus' really simple job description for apostolic workers? Here it is again: "*Go and make disciples of all nations, baptizing them in the name of the Father and of the Son and of the Holy Spirit, and **teaching them to obey everything I have commanded you.***" (Matthew 28:19-20, NIV. Emphasis mine—obviously, since Matthew's word processor didn't have bold or underline.) I've seen ministries around the world blossom that sought to truly teach obedience to Him. And I've seen many that didn't put an emphasis on that fall flat.

True confession: I grew up with a defective understanding of what Jesus actually taught. In my Protestant/Evangelical/Charismatic/Bible-based upbringing, it was something like this: "Believe in Jesus as the Son of God, accept God's forgiveness in Christ, and make Him your Lord and Savior." Now that's all good stuff. But the implication was: that's it. If one seriously seeks to live by God's ways and God's character, that's nice but not really indispensable. Sort of extra credit, like doing the extra book report in grade school over the weekend. A subtle yet powerful problem in Evangelicalism is how almost everything is seen through the prism of what gets a person into heaven. Jesus talked a little bit about that, but most of his teaching was actually about how we are to think and how to live our lives.

Embrace obedience

We live today in a milieu of disdain for authority, so nothing seems so wrong as the notion that I need to obey someone. But isn't that exactly what Jesus taught it meant to be His follower or disciple? As Dallas Willard put it,

> Discipleship affirms the unity of the present-day Christian with those who walked beside Jesus during His incarnation. To be His disciple then was to be with Him, to learn to be like Him. It was to be His student or apprentice in kingdom living. His disciples heard what He said and observed what He did, then, under His direction, they simply began to say and do the same things. They did so *imperfectly but progressively*. As he taught: 'Everyone who is fully trained will be like his teacher' (Luke 6:40, emphasis added).[29]

David Watson put it well: "God's love language to us is mercy and grace. Our love language to God is loving obedience."[30] Consider these often overlooked passages:

> "Not everyone who says to me, 'Lord, Lord,' will enter the kingdom of heaven, but only he who does the will of my Father who is in heaven." (Matthew 7:21)

> [15] "If you love me, you will obey what I command... 21 Whoever has my commands and obeys them, he is the one who loves me. He who loves me will be loved by my Father, and I too will love him and show myself to him... [23] If anyone loves me, he will obey my teaching. My Father will love him, and we will come to him and make our home with him. [24] He who does not love me will not obey my teaching." (John 14:15, 21, 23-24)

> "If you obey my commands, you will remain in my love, just as I have obeyed my Father's commands and remain in his love." (John 15:10)

This verse reminds me of Elizabeth Elliot: "When obedience to God contradicts what I think will give me pleasure, let me ask myself if I love Him."

> "[3] We know that we have come to know him if we obey his commands. [4] The man who says, "I know him," but does not do what he commands is a liar, and the truth is not in him. [5] But if anyone obeys his word, God's love is truly made complete in him. This is how we know we are in him: [6] Whoever claims to live in him must walk as Jesus did." (1 John 2:3-6)

Is this not what it means to enter the Kingdom of God and live in the Kingdom of God? [The Kingdom of God is mentioned 142 times in the New Testament!] The Kingdom of Heaven[31] is future, but He taught us that it is also very much present. If I am a citizen of a kingdom, it implicitly means I'm under the authority of the king. And throughout the gospels we are told that this restorative aligning with God's ways is good news. How did the 1st century disciples see this theme as good news and not bad news? It probably helped that they weren't 21st century Westerners with an inbred rebellious streak. G.K. Chesterton writes in *Orthodoxy*, "And the more I considered Christianity, the more I found that while it had established a rule and order, the chief aim of that order was to give room for good things to run wild."[32]

All this obedience stuff can cause a dissonance to our fiercely independent ears. But clearly it's what it means to follow Him. And if we arrive on the field with a hollowed out notion of this, we will do a disservice to those whom we disciple. But if we and they learn to obey everything which He commanded us, imperfectly but progressively, the world gets changed. Accept no substitute.

---

1. https://www.goodreads.com/quotes/33993-you-can-count-the-seeds-in-an-apple-but-you
2. https://quotationcelebration.wordpress.com/2018/01/29/though-you-can-easily-count-the-seeds-in-an-apple-its-impossible-to-count-the-apples-in-a-seed/.
3. Dick Scoggins and I—using my other penname, James Rockford—co-authored this in the 1990s. I developed the subject further in "The Pioneer Church Planting Phases," Chapter 5 in Sinclair, *A Vision of the Possible*.
4. Garrison, David. *Church Planting Movements*. Bangalore: Wigtake Resources, 2003.
5. "What is a CPM?" by Stan Parks, Chapter 6 in Parks & Coles, *24:14 – A Testimony*.
6. Trousdale, Jerry. *Miraculous Movements: How Hundreds of Thousands of Muslims Are Falling in Love with Jesus*. Nashville: Thomas Nelson, 2012, 17-18.
7. E.g. T4T (*training for trainers*); Four Fields; Zume.
8. Source withheld for security reasons.
9. Hesselgrave, David J. *Planting Churches Cross-Culturally: North America and Beyond*, 2nd ed. Grand Rapids, MI: Baker Book House, 2000. Pp.42-51.
10. www.desiringgod.org and various social media.
11. "The bare essentials of helping groups become churches" by Steve Smith, Chapter 10 in Parks & Coles. *24:14 - A Testimony*.
12. However, experience has shown that it is important for the apostolic workers to have relationships with at least some in the first to third generations.
13. Evangelistic approaches may vary. DMM emphasizes brief *"shema"* statements as spiritual hooks, to discern who's interested in more. Others will look for opportunities to share deeper (e.g. a fuller testimony, or Creation to Christ presentation).
14. I have heard David Watson of CityTeam International say that this usually happens only 15-20% of the time. Still, that's not bad.
15. Such groups are thus "second generation."
16. Source withheld for security reasons.
17. Scott Hamilton was a childhood friend of my wife's.

18. "Scott Hamilton Was Demoted as an Olympic Broadcaster. Don't Feel Sorry for Him." By Juliet Macur in *The New York Times*. 18 February 2018.
19. "Creation to Christ" is a resource made available by Training for Trainers and can be accessed here: http://t4tonline.org/wp-content/uploads/2011/02/2-Creation-to-Christ-Story.pdf.
20. The Kingdom Circles is a resource used to help visualize the Kingdom of God and our relationship to it. It is described in "Insider Movements: Honoring God-Given Identity and Community" by Rebecca Lewis in *International Journal of Frontier Missiology* 26:1 January-March) 2009:35.
21. Dent, Don. *Decisive Discipleship: Why Rapid Discipleship Is Preferable and How It Is Possible*. www.GlobalMissiology.org. October 2015.
22. John, Victor. *Bhojpuri Breakthrough: A Movement that Keeps Multiplying*. WIGTake Resources, 2019.
23. This would be a good place for me to recommend David Garrison's encouraging *A Wind in the House of Islam: How God is drawing Muslims around the world to faith in Jesus Christ*. Monument, CO: WIGTake Resources, 2014. This is a survey of movements in the Muslim world.
24. *The Chosen* is multi-season, crowd-funded video episode-series depiction of the life of Jesus available by downloading the app *The Chosen* from either the App Store or Google Play.
25. Source withheld for security reasons.
26. Jerry Trousdale, *Miraculous Movements*, 90.
27. Daniel Sinclair, *A Vision of the Possible*, 55-87.
28. You can read more about David Watson and his impact on DBS and DMM in David Watson and Paul Watson, *Contagious Disciple Making: Leading Others on a Journey of Discovery*, Nashville TN: Thomas Nelson Publishing, 2014.
29. Introduction to Houston, James. *The Prayer: Deepening Your Friendship with God*. David C. Cook, 2007.
30. Watson, David & Watson, Paul. *Contagious Disciple Making: Leading Others on a Journey of Discovery*. Nashville TN: Thomas Nelson, 2014.
31. Synonymous with the Kingdom of God.
32. Chesterton, G. K. *Orthodoxy*. Peabody, MA: Hendrickson, 2006, p. 91.

5

TIME STEWARDSHIP ON THE FIELD

> Confusion that never stops
> The closing walls and the ticking clocks gonna
> Come back and take you home
> I could not stop, that you now know, singing
> Come out upon my seas
> Cursed missed opportunities am I
> A part of the cure
> Or am I part of the disease
>
> — Clocks, by Coldplay

"This time, like all times, is a very good one, if we but know what to do with it."

— Ralph Waldo Emerson

Few of us need to be convinced that how we use our time will make a huge difference in all aspects of life. Success or failure. Fruitfulness or aimlessness. We innately sense that it's not just a matter of our work or our ministry. How we use our time affects all of life: our health (physically, mentally, and spiritually), our relationships (with spouses, children, teammates, and friends), and simply whether or not we feel good about life. Do we go for the Netflix championship in binge-watching, or actually accomplish much that is useful and fulfilling? It's up to us.

The number of books out there about "time management" may exceed the seconds of the day (86,400). Not just secular books—but stacks of Christian books as well. The lessons of this chapter, however, are **just for you**: church planters on the field, in apostolic ministry to unreached peoples. The many ways we must deal with time issues are unique and can be strange. The challenges we face as field workers are special, the decisions not always easy.

Relax - Focus - Create - Reduce – Unwind - Consecrate

We are calling this extraordinarily important area of life "time stewardship" rather than "time management." What's the difference? The latter implies merely following a set of techniques and systems, usually at a granular level of detail, in order to succeed at your job. **Stewardship** includes some of that. But the word encompasses a much broader, and more spiritual, meaning—living our days and years in a way that pleases God, and being used by Him in the purposes He has for our lives. The apostle Paul was writing about stewardship when he wrote to the Ephesians: "For we are his workmanship, created in Christ Jesus for good works, which God prepared beforehand, that we should walk in them" (Ephesians 2:10). That is a very motivating verse. The Merriam-Webster dictionary defines stewardship as "the conducting, supervising, or managing of something, **especially** the careful and responsible management of something entrusted to one's care." Imagine the Wine Steward in a Michelin 3-star restaurant. Or the head flight attendant on a flight to Tokyo. Working multi-dimensionally toward excellence. The word in New Testament Greek is *oikonomia*, which is related to our modern English word *economy*. "It is relating to the task of an *oikonos* (steward) in household administration *stewardship*, management;" and "figuratively... of the apostolic office in God's redemptive work task, responsibility, trusteeship."[1] One is reminded of Jesus' parables of purposefully entrusting financial resources to the three stewards: the *minas* (Luke 19:11-27) and the *talents* (Matthew 25:14-30). As aspiring good stewards, we endeavor, however inconsistently and imperfectly, to live our lives **now** so that when we meet the Lord **later**, we hear His personal commendation: "Well done, good and faithful servant. You have been faithful over a little; I will set you over much. Enter into the joy of your master" (Matthew 25:21). Make no mistake about it! **Time stewardship** is an immensely spiritual matter.

Stewardship also implies **opportunity**. While we are still drawing breath, we have opportunity to serve the Lord, to bless his people, and to seek to advance his purposes on earth. The time will come for all of us when we no longer have such opportunity. No one will regret in heaven any of their efforts to serve the Lord during their earthly lives. But there may be much regret for not having taken up those opportunities.

At this point, you might be fearing that this chapter's aim is to help you tweak your schedule, be more efficient, get maximum benefit from the latest technological tools, and enable you to relentlessly squeeze every possible advantage out of every minute in the day. Wow—just writing that sentence makes me feel a bit overwhelmed. No, that's not exactly the plan.

Before we jump in, permit us to be slightly philosophical: What is **time** anyway? Here are a few statements from Albert Einstein on the subject: "The only reason for time is so that everything doesn't happen at once."[2] "Time and space are modes by which we think and not conditions in which we live."[3] "The distinction between the past, present and future is only a stubbornly persistent illusion."[4] He was convinced by the math that time is not the rigid conveyor-belt of our existence we imagine it to be.

Similarly perhaps, Eckhart Tolle, author of the mega-seller *The Power of Now*, was asked "Without a sense of time, how would we function in this world?...I think Time is something very precious and we need to learn to use it wisely rather than waste it." His reply is stunning: "Time isn't precious at all, because it is an illusion." and "In the absence of time, all your problems dissolve." He even postulates that "Eternity, of course, does not mean endless time, but no time."[5]

Hmmm. Something to think about anyway—though I don't think the Bible solves that riddle for us. Even Christian teachings on **mindfulness**[6] urge us against a preoccupation with the clock. This conception of time is not hard to find in Sufism, Buddhism and New Age. So is that how it is?

As Christians, should we reject the atheistic approach of Einstein, or the philosophies found in various forms of pantheism? Some of these other ways of thinking may contain helpful truths, and after all, all truth is God's truth. But in Scripture time is neither a delusion nor unimportant. At the same time many passages draw us away from compulsive over-attention to the hours or days, or of being hung up on the past or the future. We need a balanced perspective. So while time may not necessarily be the ultimate commodity of value to be slavish about, how we *steward* the eight facets of life below ("Life Skills") will make a huge difference. **That's what this chapter is about.**

A generalization in psychology is that depressed people spend too much time thinking about the past, anxious people are always planning or problem-solving for the future, but healthy people spend most of their time mentally and emotionally in the present. We need

Calm - Serenity - Composure

So what should our mindset be—led by Scripture—on this absolutely vital aspect of life?

First of all, how we spend our time is very much addressed in the Bible. Consider:

- Psalm 90:12 *So teach us to number our days that we may get a heart of wisdom.*
- *Moses spoke of having 70-80 years in life. We all need a realistic picture of how much longer we may have left, and prioritize in light of that.*
- Proverbs 6:6-9 *Go to the ant, O sluggard; consider her ways, and be wise. Without having any chief, officer, or ruler, she prepares her bread in summer and gathers her food in harvest. How long*

will you lie there, O sluggard? When will you arise from your sleep?
- Proverbs 21:5 *The plans of the diligent lead surely to abundance, but everyone who is hasty comes only to poverty.*
- Mark 13:34 *It is like a man going on a journey, when he leaves home and puts his servants in charge, each with his work, and commands the doorkeeper to stay awake.*
- [This is part of Jesus' last teaching to his followers before going to the Cross. For the rest of our lives on Earth each one of us will have "his work," his stewardship from the Lord.]
- Ephesians 5:15-17 *Look carefully then how you walk, not as unwise but as wise, making the best use of the time, because the days are evil. Therefore do not be foolish, but understand what the will of the Lord is.*

From the standpoint of Scripture, how we order our days and steward our time is even more important than how we use our money. Even the word 'wisdom'—so prevalent in Proverbs—basically means **the skill of living**, which includes our priorities, values, decisions, and heart commitments. In a sense, how we use our time is where all the various threads of life come together in practical everyday ways. Does that sound like pressure? It needn't be. This chapter is aimed at lessening your overall burden, not adding to it.

What areas of life are likely impacted? Specifically we will discuss these two or three spheres: One's ministry and **tentmaking**, if that applies (see below), as well as one's personal life and relationships.

When you as a field worker apply the principles, priorities and tools shared in this chapter, you can expect to experience these benefits:

- An ability to relax;
- Improved focus and a clearer mind;
- Creativity in your work;
- Being better able to keep the bigger picture in view and remain vision-driven;
- Staying Bible-centered;

- Investing more in important things, and being less at the mercy of the *tyranny-of-the-urgent*;
- An ability to make strategic mid-course changes;
- Defeating confusion, anxiety, and feeling overwhelmed;
- Feeling comfortable regarding what you are NOT getting done, especially if we get a sense that something must not be the Lord's *yoke* for us (Matthew 11:28-30).

WHO DOESN'T WANT THESE THINGS?

We will examine eight life skills that will help make you wise and fruitful in spiritual time stewardship. As you examine the life skills, it will help to not view them as separate compartments, but rather as eight facets of a single diamond, eight aspects of your personal time *ecosystem*.

Life Skill #1: Differentiating 'Work' from 'Personal'

Some personalities are really drawn to distinctions and borders and categories. Others have an aversion to such things. I know people who, from the moment their eyes open in the morning until their heads hit their pillows at night, experience life as one seamless cloth of whatever comes their way. The days are filled from one end to the other with ministry, phone calls, getting caught up on social media, emails, a language lesson, a team meeting, relationships, meals, brushing teeth, teaching or learning, reading, getting their tires rotated, praying, spending time in the Word, exercising, watching TV, washing dishes, resting, staring at the wall, trying with aggravation to get the computer to behave, thinking through all the people in their lives and how they might bless them, and so on. With this approach it's all a mix, a hodgepodge, an undifferentiated flow of this and that.

Some of you are thinking. "What's so wrong with that? Especially for real spontaneous types? It even sounds kind of spiritual." Whatever we think, we've all experienced that there are certainly days or even weeks on the field when it is that way, no matter how much we might try to get a handle on things. We're at the helm trying to steer the ship, but someone has disconnected the tiller from the rudder. Despite our best efforts, we are out of control and aren't sure we are getting anywhere.

In contrast, some overly structured types may need to learn how to relax more and be more spontaneous. Either way, I believe that for all of us on the field, to not differentiate is a recipe for burnout and for a bad family life.[7] Let's talk now about making some distinctions between your work/ministry life and being in "personal mode." Just as God's six days of creation and His rest on the seventh day/Sabbath were greatly differentiated, so too God has wired us in a way that we need to manage different facets of life in different ways. Let's have a look at three areas:

Ministry

This category involves everything directly involved in working toward why we came to a new culture, to help people follow Christ and to accomplish church-planting (movements). These would include relationship-building with those we're seeking to reach, sharing Christ, discipling, language-learning, team life and meetings, prayer—individually and with others—teaching the Word, and so much more.

Tentmaking

By "tentmaking," we generally mean a visible vocational role one may have in society for the sake of residency, viability, access, and perhaps income. Generally this would be a job, a business, a humanitarian project, or pursuing a graduate degree. See Life Skill #6 below. For many of us, this can be very time-consuming, sometimes in a good way and other times not so much. But in the economy of life it includes all the hours involved working at that vocation, including preparations. In a way, as tentmaking is a means toward ministry ends, it is a subset of ministry. And ideally there can be much overlap between the two. Oftentimes there are good times with nationals on the job, working in the local language, opportunities to disciple, etc. In other words, hopefully the hours one invests in his or her job, business, NGO, or whatever is not just what one HAS to do to be in the country but is redemptive. You may wish to view your ministry sphere as distinct from your tentmaking life, or it may serve you better to see them as one. This is why sometimes in this chapter we've mentioned three spheres, and at other times two spheres, i.e. two for those who want to view ministry and tentmaking united as one sphere. Choose whichever approach suits you best.

Personal

This is everything else you do in life: Sleeping, eating, resting, time with family, doing whatever you do for fun, days off, shampooing your hair, time in the car, getting that car fixed at the mechanic, pursuing a hobby, staying in touch with family back home, taking out the trash, going to the gym, fixing a broken lamp, one's personal daily **Quiet Times** (see below), or those rare moments when you are just doing nothing.

I truly believe the Lord can make you successful in both spheres of life: You can flourish in ministry/tentmaking as well as all aspects of your personal and family life. We err if we think it's got to be either/or, or make it a hierarchy of one automatically trumping the other.

Why should we make a distinction?

Clearly these two or three spheres of your life are very different from each other. On the job, it may all be about hard work and steady, measurable accomplishments. Ministry often involves investing many hours building relationships, which is harder to measure. It involves things like getting more into the culture and nurturing team life. With these things, we don't typically just tick off tasks. Often the best and most strategic things we need to do won't make us feel "efficient." Nonetheless hard work and risk are often involved (see Romans 15:3, 6, 9, 12, 21). And as we've said, the personal sphere is normally quite different. Normally I even judge the success of a day off by how much I didn't do. The point is, we have to make distinctions between ministry, tentmaking and personal because these three spheres are very different in nature. How we "manage" or approach or prosper in one sphere is different than how we operate in the others, and there must be a healthy balance between them. And we must be able to effectively switch gears between them.

We need to protect our personal lives. When field kids are chronically neglected because of the ministry, it's heartbreaking. When marriages on the field break up, it's tragic. Without some kind of balance, severe strains between couples, anxiety, depression, spiritual dryness and burnout aren't far away. You see, this is why **time stewardship** is about more than mere time-efficiencies. It's about life. I've seen field couples close to break up, and at the root of it were obvious problems in their time stewardship, and how that negatively impacted other facets of their lives in negative ways.

Likewise, wouldn't it be great that when you are "off," you are really "off"? For example, let's hope that when you are playing with the kiddos, your heart is free to be with them, rather than your thoughts being stuck on that prayer letter that desperately needs writing. You always want to be focused on what you should be focused on at the time.

On the other side of the coin, we need to be "workers approved by God" (2 Timothy 2:15), engaged regularly in serious, earnest ministry of various kinds. We need to be able to consistently jump in with focus, dedication and energy, as the Lord enables by His Holy Spirit. I remember visiting a family on a team in our organization in Central Asia. The lack of good time stewardship was threatening to end this couple's field career. Both husband and wife based all their activities from home—neither had a workplace to go or outside ministry setting. As homeschoolers, all four kids were also at home all the time. I was struck how their lives were a mosaic of constant interruptions, mostly just about survival matters: shopping, fixing, cleaning, cooking, etc. Later when I shared my observations and concerns to the team leader, he said, "Yes, I know. I've been desperately trying to engage with them, to find solutions, and help them steward their time to make real progress in language and relationships. But it's not working. They're not taking it seriously. We'll probably have to send them home."

Only by viewing and managing the two or three spheres differently can we correct overwork or underwork extremes. In some places—especially where the tentmaking demands are high—this isn't so much an issue, as your discretionary time is quite limited. But see Life Skills #6 and #7 below. In some situations, people can fall into "underwork." More common however, is seeing workers burning the candle at both ends, and a bit in the middle too. Later in the chapter, we'll address these issues; but it starts by grasping how the different realms are different and need to be handled differently.[8]

Making the distinctions also helps to get spouses together on the same page, enabling the necessary conversations to take place. Believe me, if you don't do it, tensions are inevitable. Work things through, and the tensions should subside.

Finally, perceiving and managing the different areas of your time in a balanced way will help you not fall into the trap of undeserved guilt. It is said that we overestimate what we can do in the short-run, and underestimate what we can accomplish in the long-run. Unfortunately we are often emotionally focused on the short-term, and so we feel overwhelmed about all the things we are not getting to: "I'm not learning the language well enough, I fear we may lose donors because of our inadequate communications, there are five key relationships I could easily pursue but have time only for two this month, and our prayer meetings are too short. Add to this that our child is failing Arabic in school, the house is a mess, and my tentmaking business is losing money. Ugggh." But if I have a semblance of priorities and balance from the Lord—no one gets it perfect(!)—I can begin to renounce those feelings of failure and guilt, knowing He who brought me here is faithful. From me He only requires faithfulness. And we rest in the knowledge that any spiritual fruit will ultimately be His doing. Simply obedience is success.

How Can This Work?

Consider your stage of life.

I will point out something that should be obvious. There are different seasons of life, and how we deal with these issues will vary a lot between people at different stages. Imagine the young single, or young couple without kids, newly arrived on the field and focused primarily on language-learning. Then there is the less *young* or middle-aged family: parents in their early-40s, four kids over a span of ages, innumerable activities, and child-raising challenges, just like there would be back in the home country. But add to that the additional layers of cross-cultural complexities, a 45-hour tentmaking workweek, and perhaps the added responsibility of leading a team or even some regional responsibilities. Yikes! Eons ago I had a small business for many years in Jordan. It was a blessing, an arena for ministry, and at times quite a heavy load. Can you survive? Even thrive? Yes. Been there, done that. Got the T-shirt. And am here to talk about it.

And, of course, there are older couples or singles whose kids have flown the nest. That's us. Our local friends are not in their 20s or 30s, but older, grandparents like us. We're now in a different Middle East country and enjoying a more flexible, less time-demanding visa situation. That's good, since I don't have the energy I had in my 30s!

Put up a curtain, not a wall

Even if you have a semi-normal job, business or routine, life on the field is not the same as back in your home country. Even if you have a 9-to-5 job, you must have a lot of flexibility in how you roll, in how activities may flow into the other. Am I now contradicting myself? Not really. I'm just suggesting that the mental and practical separation between Ministry and Personal should not be viewed as a **wall** but more as a **curtain**—some flexibility; not absolutely rigid. You may be getting up from the dinner table and about to rest a bit, and then your phone rings and it's a local friend you've been really praying for. You chat for a bit, then he gets serious. He wants to know if the prophets are the same as normal people or not. What do you do? You flex.

How long is a "workweek"?

But let's talk about your Ministry/Tentmaking workweek. There are 168 hours in the week. There's no app that can make that 198 hours—thankfully. And if you have around eight hours per night for sleep and all your bedtime routines, that leaves 112 hours. That may sound like a lot, but with all of life's essential activities, it can easily feel like it's not enough. Here's the deal: You are forced by that limitation to be thoughtful and strategic in how you spend your time, and **that is actually a good thing**. One hundred and twelve waking hours. That total can flex some, but not much.[9] It's sort of like the proverbial large glass jar, in which you have to fit into it large rocks, smaller rocks, and sand. Prioritize and plan. None of us want to be busy but unfruitful.

Many years ago, I was asked to leave Jordan and move to England with my family to take on the role of Field Director in our organization. Prayerfully, and with some reluctance, we agreed and made the big move. There were many changes and adjustments: The weather was cloudy and rainy, our home was smaller, we needed two cars instead of one, our kids could walk to (free) school across the street, and everything was in English. I no longer had a tentmaking business to run, but the new responsibilities were overwhelming. I was 38 years old and responsible for the oversight of 75 teams (over 400 gospel workers, plus about as many kids, in some of the world's most dangerous places), from Mauritania to Mindanao and everything in-between in the 10/40 Window. The position involved heavy travel. I could see that I could easily be crushed by it all. In fact, after a couple months into the job, I experienced a mini-breakdown. Couldn't sleep or even get out of bed for a couple days.

So my wife Liz and I decided that I would maintain a reasonable schedule and routine when I wasn't traveling, and we would stick with that. I would give it a certain number of hours per week, with a somewhat consistent schedule, and do a minimum of work at home. We were able to have dinner together as a family most nights. We decided on a certain size of "ministry jar," and what would fit would fit, and what would not fit simply wouldn't get done, and that was OK. It's very popular these days to talk about setting life boundaries and margins. That's what we were doing, even though we didn't really know the concept or jargon at the time.

That turned out to be the best decision we could possibly make at the beginning of this new challenging chapter in our lives. That forced me to think strategically about what I could realistically do and what I could take on within a limited amount of time each week. I would go after those things with vigor and creativity, and not feel badly if I couldn't get to other things. If I had had only a vague sense of how much time and energy there was for the ministry, I would not have been forced to do that strategic planning, and no doubt my marriage, parenting and personal life would have all suffered, with urgent field things constantly hijacking every waking moment.

But again, it begins by perceiving the two or three arenas differently, and mentally drawing the lines of separation between them, and then it's easier to manage them appropriately. Let's get into some specifics.

Life Skill #2: Prioritizing Personal Quiet Times

Please set aside 30-40 minutes to read this section slowly in its entirety. Then pray about how the Lord would have you respond. It's too important to rush through.

When I was 15, growing up in a little town in the Central Valley of California, I got very involved in a Christian coffee house. Though I was from a respectable and sheltered background, most of the others there had rough pasts, like recovering from drug addictions. It was a block from the railroad tracks, in a seedy part of town. We would often go out witnessing on the streets. Once a biker was so bothered by the message that he threatened to kill me.

One night we had a special speaker all the way from Fresno. He was from a very charismatic denomination and looked like a television evangelist. He wore a brightly colored shirt with most of the buttons open, tight bell-bottomed pants, and a wide white belt with matching shiny white shoes. It seemed he must have spent at least an hour getting his hair just right. It was, after all, the early 70s. But you just never know the instruments God will use to send us powerful messages. He said something that night that changed my life. "Kids, you should all really consider spending some time every day in fellowship with God: praying and being in His word." He explained that this was not a pride thing nor to earn heavenly points, but rather it was to experience Him more deeply, and that no other investment of time would ever be more valuable. At first this struck me as crazy, impractical, and unsustainable. But I couldn't get it out of my head. Soon, I gave it a try, and I haven't looked back for 49 years.

The key point of this Life Skill #2 is that regardless of whatever else is going on, we don't take shortcuts with vital spiritual priorities like our quiet times.

Sometimes called "daily devotions," having a "quiet time" is probably still the most common term for this sort of thing. Generations ago they called these "vespers." I like that: "I'm having my vespers." But we'll stick with calling this practice a quiet time. The idea is simple—to have a regular pattern of reading the Bible and praying nearly every day.[10] The amount of time you spend on a quiet time is perhaps less important than its consistency. While some find that the end of the day is good, or even in the middle, most find that the first thing in the day is best for them. Do whatever works best for you. Of course, more important than **when** or even **what** you do in your quiet time, the precious thing is that you are focused on connecting with the Lord in His presence. There are times when it is the high point of the day, and you really look forward to the next time. And there are other times you really don't feel like it. But you press on in spiritual discipline,[11] trusting that no other activity of the day is more important, and that it yields wonderful fruit in our lives over time. In fact, this exercise of self-control is part of what the Apostle Paul called "the fruit of the Spirit." (Galatians 5:23) Persisting when you don't feel like it is a healthy act of faith that pleases the Lord. And while all this is important for every believer, it is especially vital for those called to earnest ministry.

Without faith it is impossible to please him, for whoever would draw near to God must believe that he exists and that he rewards those who seek him (Hebrews 11:6). Let's go for it!

Delighting in the Word in Our Daily Lives - A Sampling

[David's charge to Solomon] [*Walk*] *in his ways and* [*keep*] *his statutes, his commandments, his rules, and his testimonies, as it is written in the Law of Moses, that you may prosper in all that you do...* (1 Kings 2:3).

[Why Ezra was so powerfully used by God] *For on the first day of the first month he began to go up from Babylonia, and on the first day of the fifth month he came to Jerusalem, for the good hand of his God was on him. For Ezra had set his heart to study the Law of the LORD, and to do it and to teach his statutes and rules in Israel* (Ezra 7:9-10).

As the Lord can choose anyone He wants to use, it makes sense that He rewards and uses leaders who are committed to His Word.

*...but his delight is in the law of the LORD, and **on his law he meditates day and night**. He is like a tree planted by streams of water that yields its fruit in its season, and its leaf does not wither. In all that he does, he prospers* (Psalm 1:2-3).

A powerful picture to open up the Psalter. The way to prosper in all aspects of life is to walk with God on the basis of His Word (*torah*). "Day and night" point to consistency of practice.

But [Jesus] answered, "It is written, 'Man shall not live by bread alone, but by every word that comes from the mouth of God'" (Matthew 4:4, quoting Deut. 8:3).

Taking in and living by God's Word is more important than anything else in life. Christ's emphasis on "every word" is interesting, i.e. even the little details matter a lot.

If you abide in my word, *you are truly my disciples, and you will know the truth, and the truth will set you free* (John 8:31-32).

As we'll see further throughout this chapter, we need to be set free in various ways. God's Word plays a vital part of this process.

And he stayed a year and six months, teaching the word of God among them (Acts 18:11).

A pithy one-line description Luke gives to sum up everything Paul did in Corinth for a year and a half. Luke and Paul saw everything he did there in the context of teaching the Word.

[Paul to the Ephesian elders] *...for I did not shrink from declaring to you* **the whole counsel of God** (Acts 20:27).

[Paul to Timothy] *Do your best to present yourself to God as one approved, a* **worker** *who has no need to be ashamed,* **rightly handling the word of truth** (2 Timothy 2:15).

It's almost a cliché that we minister out of the overflow of our walk with God, and this also applies vitally to our Word-life.

All Scripture is breathed out by God and profitable for teaching, for reproof, for correction, and for training in righteousness, that the man of God may be competent, equipped for every good work (2 Timothy 3:16-17).

There's no better all-encompassing description of how we get equipped for fruitfulness.

As each has received a gift, use it to serve one another, as good stewards of God's varied grace: whoever speaks, as one who speaks oracles of God... (1 Peter 4:10-11).

Obviously if we are to **speak for God** in our speaking ministries, Scripture should deeply rooted in our lives.

*...like newborn babies, **long for the pure milk of the word**, so that by it you may grow in respect to salvation...* (1 Peter 2:2 NASB).[12]

The Prayer Life of the Believer – A Sampling

There are 322 occurrences of 'pray' in the Bible, in various forms.

The entire book of Psalms teaches us about prayer, and how central it is in the life of the YHWH-follower.

*Let my **prayer** be counted as incense before you, and the lifting up of my hands as the evening sacrifice!* (Psalm 141:2).

*But **when you pray**, go into your room and shut the door and pray to your Father who is in secret. And your Father who sees in secret will reward you* (Matthew 6:6).

And after he had dismissed the crowds, he went up on the mountain by himself to pray. When evening came, he was there alone... (Matthew 14:23).

An evening **quiet time**.

And whatever you ask in prayer, you will receive, if you have faith (Matthew 21:22).

Who doesn't want that?

And rising very early in the morning, while it was still dark, he departed and went out to a desolate place, and there he prayed (Mark 1:35).

A morning **quiet time**. And numerous other instances of Jesus going off to pray by himself. Raise your hand if the Son of God, full of the Holy Spirit, needed a consistent and vibrant prayer life with the Father, and you feel we somehow we need it less?

[The priorities of the Apostles] *But we will devote ourselves to prayer and to the ministry of the word* (Acts 6:4).

[Cornelius]...*a devout man who feared God with all his household, gave alms generously to the people, and prayed* **continually** *to God* (Acts 10:2).

And so, from the day we heard, **we have not ceased to pray for you,** *asking that you may be filled with the knowledge of his will in all spiritual wisdom and understanding...* (Colossians 1:9)

Continue steadfastly in prayer, *being watchful in it with thanksgiving* (Colossians 4:2).

...*pray without ceasing!* (1 Thessalonians 5:17).

And when he had taken the scroll, the four living creatures and the twenty-four elders fell down before the Lamb, each holding a harp, and golden bowls full of incense, **which are the prayers of the saints** (Revelation 5:8).

So What Are We to Make of All This?

There is nothing more significant in your life than to know Christ, to commune with Him throughout the day, and to grow ever deeper with Him. That's what Paul means when he refers to "the surpassing worth of knowing Christ Jesus my Lord." Everything else for him was as "rubbish,"[13] which is a dramatic way of saying it is much less important. Less than **secondary**. Our Word-life and our prayer-life are the key arenas in which we fellowship with God. What else deserves a higher priority in our lives? Nothing.

Is this about our edification and fellowship with God, or about equipping us for fruitful ministry? For the man or woman in ministry, it's clearly both. But beware the trap of only being in the Word as you prepare for teaching. Time in the Word as an avenue for connecting with God is more important than studying to get our notes ready.

Ministry not done in the Holy Spirit and in dependency on God is worthless activity. Is this not why Jesus went deep in prayer at every juncture in His life and work?

What about our motivations? Ahh, now we're getting to the tricky bits. Is it possible to institute in one's life regular **quiet times** for the wrong motives? Out of pride? Or giving in to a guilt-trip? Or to somehow better merit God's love and salvation? Or to increase your head-knowledge in order to impress others with your spirituality? **Yes to all the above.** Through the centuries all His saints have had to wrestle with motives. That's why it's essential we regularly crucify all such unworthy intentions. As someone has said, if you find yourself doing the right thing for the wrong motive, change your motive. "For where your treasure is, there your heart will be also" (Matthew 6:21). We then enjoy time with God, in the Holy Spirit, in an attitude of humble seeking.

Some Practical Bits

Most of us understand how vitally important this is, but some struggle with HOW to actually make it work. If that's you, consider asking a friend to help you think through how to connect with God regularly and creatively, in a way that fits you. Here are some *Quiet Time hacks*.

- **Schedule It.** Does the Bible teach that all our activity in prayer and Scripture should be encapsulated in one daily block of time? Of course not. Praying without ceasing, for example, implies communication with the Lord throughout the day. But some of the verses do imply the practice of a consistent and focused time with the Lord, daily, or nearly so.[14] For most of us, if it's not in our schedules, it doesn't happen.
- **How long?** I recommend that people decide how long to spend in *quiet time* with the Lord on a daily basis, figure out

where that is going to fit best in your schedule, and launch out. Of course, all of that can and probably will be adjusted.
- **"Quiet."** It's important that it be as uninterrupted as possible. Quiet place. Phones off. Those around us knowing it's not a good time to talk to us. Etc. Husbands and wives, especially with young kids around, will want to coordinate to regularly give each other that kind of time. Who wouldn't want their spouse to have close time with the Lord?
- **Variety.** Prayer, of course, is not one-dimensional. All that I've written above is meant to include all the many rich aspects of prayer. It's so multi-faceted. These include thanksgiving, worship (in song or not), reflection, confession, petition (for ourselves and for others), even complaining.[15] Many have a precious time in just being silent before God, or **listening prayer**.
- Likewise, there can be different ways to be in the Word. My two favorite are slow, careful reading (usually using a study Bible with running commentary, and journaling insights I get); and in-depth study of a passage.[16] There are also times in which I'll just be sitting quietly, pondering a verse or section or topic, and then I'll get a flood of insights.
- **Bring it into you.** The Old Testament talks a lot about **meditation** (or reflection); and memorization is implied. Indeed, it is only in relatively recent times that believers have their own copies of the Bible. Until then, most were dependent on hearing teaching, memorizing the books or passages, and meditating on what they had. Since we have all of Scripture in our hands, it should be at least that good. Same principles apply.

So dear reader: Do you have a consistent, life-giving, quiet time practice? How would the Lord have you respond to these exhortations? What changes do you plan to make?

Life Skill #3: Dealing with Your E-Communications

A long time ago in a galaxy not so far away, communicating with friends, family and work colleagues was simpler. If you needed to interact with another human being about something, you could almost always just pick up the phone and **dial** their number. It normally worked fine. There were only two possible complications with this use of technology: a) They might have two different numbers (home and work); and b) They might not actually be there. If they weren't around, that would trigger the next low-tech "app": You would leave a message for them. In later technologies, a sophisticated person might actually own an answering machine. And if someone was across the country, you could still call them—it just might not be cheap. And sometimes people would actually take the radical step of putting their thoughts down on paper—by handwriting or typing—fold up the paper and put it inside another **holder** piece of paper (an envelope), and then put a small sticky piece of paper on the outside (a stamp). The recipient would get it within an amount of time reasonable for most things. Life was simple. And I didn't even mention that sometimes people would actually talk face-to-face.

When Liz and I first went out to Egypt, our only means of rapid communications available to us was the ancient Telex. To get a message quickly to someone back home in the U.S., we would craft a message, as short as possible to save cost, even eliminating unnecessary letters. Then I'd walk it over to a hotel and hand our message to the Telex operator. She would then type it into a big expensive machine, creating a long, punched tape. There would inevitably be typos, so this might take a couple iterations. When we agreed it was all ready, she would feed it through the machine again on an open international line. And it wasn't cheap. By the mid-90s, email began to be available, and life as we knew it began to change!

Radical Change and Ramifications

Now you would think that these days with our smartphones, laptops, tablets, iWatches, and car infotainment systems communicating with other people would be so much easier. Of course, in many ways, it is. I can be out in a rural area taking a walk, and on the spur of the moment have a quick video conversation on my iPhone with my grandson on another continent—for free! That's still mind-boggling. But these days, even though the person you want to communicate with may have various apps and accounts, they probably only check one or two of them regularly. So you have to know and remember: Is this a phone person (increasingly, many are not), an email person (probably older), a WhatsApp person, someone who only looks at Threema, and so on. Add to this wizardry Viber, Telegram, Facebook Messenger, iMessage, Signal, Zoom, VSee, Skype, FaceTime, Slack, Sococo, Wire, Wickr, and even a Marco Polo—and each of these have their own sign-ups and learning curves before one can be functional in them. Did I mention the antediluvian tool of sending SMS messages? There are also social media platforms such as Twitter, Bluejeans, TikTok, Instagram and Snapchat, which generally include some messaging ability. Another layer of complexity to all this is that in many of our countries, most of these apps will not work unless you first turn your VPN on, which often cuts bandwidth to a trickle. Now, if you're under 30 you're probably thinking, "Yeah, so what's the problem?!" And by the time you're reading this, this list is no doubt already out-of-date. And you Gen-Z readers are probably laughing at that list!

This topic may seem odd to be Life Skill #3. Is this important? Definitely. Even though all of these tools represent quantum leaps forward in instant communication around the world, plus encryption security, plus group collaboration, plus online meetings, there are a couple big downsides. First of all, we have begun to spend enormous amounts of time on our many screens. We use them, of course, not just for communication, but also for entertainment, banking, taking and managing our photos, keeping our calendars, and so on. When I want to just rest and read a book, even that's on a screen. Glowing rectangles! All of this is globally creating diminished attention spans and an acceleration in anxiety and depression, especially among the youth. That problem, however, is beyond the scope of this book.

Perhaps the relevant lie for gospel workers on the field with busy schedules and complex lives is the notion that everything must be answered right away. Either NOW, or perhaps a few nanoseconds from now. We hear a lot about computers and artificial intelligence. But what about the

artificial stupidity in how we've allowed all of our glowing rectangles to take over our brains? It seems that we are obligated as members-in-good-standing of the human race to answer every phone call (no matter whatever else we might be doing), and very quickly reply (within an hour?) to every WhatsApp, Threema, SMS, Messenger and Zoom call. Because email is so **last-decade**, those messages can wait some days.

The sheer volume of all these instantaneous electronic communications often creates pressure in the life and ministry of today's field worker. Sadly, people can become swallowed up by it all, expending enormous amounts of time and energy just to keep up. And to make matters worse, doing all this can create the illusion that important things are being accomplished. Sometimes they are, oftentimes not so much. Some others do the exact opposite, declaring, "I'm not going to fall into that trap. I'm going to keep my priorities right in ministry and focus on people. So I won't answer a phone call unless I see it's from someone I know I should talk to now. And I will get around to emails and WhatsApp messages eventually, when it's convenient, in the fullness of time, when I have nothing else better to do." Which means almost never. No distinction is made between important messages and trivial messages, and so all messages pile up like a tsunami, and it's too overwhelming to even get started. A brother showed me his WhatsApp app showing me 150 blue dots of the unread messages stretching back months. So everyone in his life is exasperated with him. All the while they sink under the subconscious weight, knowing that all those monsters are still out there, like an unpayable credit card balance carrying a 22% Annual Percentage Rate.

Is there a better way? Yes!

Phone Calls

The oldest technology in our list, the humble phone call is still part of the lives of some. Some of us get a lot of phone calls, while others of us don't. Your practice will depend upon the volume you receive. Please...

- **Don't be ruled by your phone.** All of us need to give ourselves the freedom or permission to not answer every phone call. For those who don't feel that freedom, it can be a bit like going through life with a chain relentlessly around your ankles. It's knowing that no matter what a special moment you're having or how restful you feel, it could all be spoiled at any moment by the cursed ringtone.

- **Focus on those you are with.** Of course, no matter how careful we are about our calls, there are some calls we need to take. But hopefully, those times are the exception and not the rule on a daily basis. In general, when it is not a good time to talk, and when the call is from someone you can call back later, we should do that. How many times have we slightly offended the people we are physically with by taking a call we didn't really need to take or, conversely, we are annoyed by someone we're with taking a call?
- **Unplug when you can.** We all need times during the day when our phones aren't even with us, so we aren't distracted, such as during our Quiet Times, while in a prayer meeting, or during a nice dinner with family.

Messaging Apps

Now let's get to a practical method for handling all the messages you receive. I recently gave a training to a large group of gospel workers who were mostly in their 20s and 30s. I asked which they received more of, emails or messages on messaging apps such as WhatsApp. I was a bit surprised to find that it was the latter. Just five years ago it would have tilted more toward emails, at least for ministry-related matters. But whether we're talking about email or WhatsApp or something totally new by the time you're reading this, the overall principles are the same, and are consistent with David Allen's bestseller *Getting Things Done: The Art of Stress-Free Productivity*.[17]

Let's imagine that Nicole receives an average of 30 messages each day. Some of these are unimportant or trivial: funny memes, group replies to replies to replies, some video she has no intention of ever watching or a link to an article she has no plan to ever read. Other messages, however, are truly important, and are from people in her life she wants to honor with timely and thoughtful responses. These are not only from family and ministry colleagues, but often from dear local friends, and keeping her presence alive in a group message can mean so much.

Here is what I suggest. Again, please...

- **Don't constantly check messages.** It's tempting to, but it is important that you maintain better focus than that.
- **Try to limit it to once a day.** Go through your new messages once a day (except maybe not at all on your Sabbath). The idea is to see what's there and have no lingering unread messages clogging up your days—those pesky blue dots.[18]
- **Apply the 3-minute rule.**[19] What's that, you say? So many messages do not warrant any response. Many you can see what it is in 5 seconds and move on. Other messages require a response. Here's how the rule works: If you can and should deal with it in 3 minutes or less, go ahead. If it's going to take more than 3 minutes, create a task for it in your Tasks System (see skill #4). That way it won't fall through the cracks, you won't need to expend any mental energy remembering that you need to get back with Joe, and you will deal with it at some point, whether sooner or later, with the appropriate level of priority. Simple! But the 3-minute rule can really help you steward your time. (You may want to reread this until it is clear for you.)
- And if you really want to watch that 8-minute super cute cat video your aunt sent you, this doesn't mean you can't. You set the priorities, but maybe you watch it later in the day when you just need to chill.
- **Set your notifications.** Go into your settings and customize your settings for notifications in a way that works for you. You don't want your phone dinging several times an hour. I leave notifications on for personal messages, and off for group messages. Others may wish to turn off all notifications.

Remember, **methods** have more than the simple purpose of not wasting time. You will recall from the Introduction above two of the outcomes we can expect from good time stewardship: "Better focus and clearer minds," and "Creativity in your work."

Emails

If you get lots of emails every day and have a hard time keeping up, then I would urge you to read Appendix 8 on handling emails. In it, I lay out a simple system that keeps you ruling over the onslaught of so many emails, rather than it ruling over you.

Note: The method and principles in that appendix also apply to electronic messaging or whatever your main inputs come from.

Let's now imagine that Nicole receives around 15 emails a day. As before, most of these are unimportant, but a few are important. As with any inflow of communications to her, she wants to deal with them quickly, not have important ones fall through the cracks, and not have to remember in her head what she needs to eventually get to. Here are some simple dos and don'ts for managing email:

- **DON'T** create folders for topics or senders. If you're unconvinced, see the Appendix for why that is an unhelpful practice.
- **DON'T** waste any time thinking about which ones to keep or delete.
- **DO** go through the new messages in your inbox once a day. Do this quickly by applying the 3-minute rule to your email (see steps above).
- **DO** sort your inbox messages. After you've gone through the inbox, DO move all those messages into your folder for the current month, titling it with the month and year.
- **DO** congratulate yourself. Enjoy that sense of satisfaction for once again having an empty inbox!

Nicole can do all this sorting in about 5 to 10 minutes a day.

Does this sound like it will be hard for you? Remember, self-control is a fruit of the Spirit. Ask for the Spirit's help as you seek to steward your time well.

Could it be that you let calls and messages absorb too much of your time and take your attention hostage? Are you prevented from being mentally free to concentrate for good periods of time on priority people and projects? Are your creativity and spontaneity healthy or suppressed? Perhaps with each phone call or message, we experience a tiny spurt of adrenaline or dopamine or something and are subconsciously reassured that we still matter in this world—we belong, we are important. But those are things we just need to trust God with, as our significance is secure in Him, and not enslave ourselves to overdoing it with e-communications.

Life Skill #4: Setting Up Your System for Work and Tasks

We are indebted to Dr. Henry Cloud for the revelation that we are sequential beings and that multi-tasking is a myth,[20] created by the psychiatric profession to make clients out of us all. OK, Cloud didn't say that last part. The reality is, however, that keeping a bunch of disconnected tasks in our heads and switching back-and-forth between them throughout the day without closure, is not a clever way to get a lot of things done in less time. Rather it is a recipe for stress and anxiety. It's even worse than that. Dr. Cal Newport warns against the frequent stimuli from social media and its giving of intermittent rewards.[21] Ominously, if large portions of your day are in a state of fragmented attention, there is potential to actually reduce your capacity for concentration permanently.

Work done in a multi-tasking mode will usually mean that what you do finish will be of lower quality. Important efforts in life and ministry require healthy concentration, and maintaining good focus is therapeutic for the brain. Therefore, we need to arrange life so that we work on things sequentially, in more or less the best priority, and without haste. Of course, bigger projects can be broken up into parts. This chapter is to help you establish the optimal system for you.

However we approach this subject, especially on the field, we need to remain 'loose,' maintaining spontaneity, avoiding machine-like rigidity, and trusting God when the unexpected comes up and throws our good plans into the weed-chopper. The one thing we can expect on the field is that the unexpected will visit us often.

As we said previously, the other reality to keep in mind when dealing with a topic such as this is that field workers are in a great variety of life situations. Some have very time-consuming tentmaking jobs, and there is not much capacity for many tasks or projects outside the workplace or beyond essential relationships. Similarly, some mothers of young children are often swamped with just getting through the day—putting the laundry into the washing machine and the kids in the bathtub—and a good day is not getting those reversed. [Important caveat: I am saying "some" mothers of young children, because the husband doing all the outside work and the wife majoring on all the family and domestic work is certainly not the only model. Many couples divide things up quite differently.] For some mothers, just doing those things and making some progress on language and relationships is quite good, and they don't see themselves taking on much more. For a few, then, a good task system isn't a high felt need.

The point is that there's no one-size fits all model, as people are in different life and ministry situations. That said, most workers are dealing with similar sets of challenges, and do need to attend effectively to things like evangelizing and discipling preparations, vital communications, Bible study, keeping their residency valid, investing some time in relationships with donors, reading or getting training, working on language skills, and rescuing a crashed laptop. Because of this, most of us would benefit from an effective **task management system. What we mean by that is what ways you use to organize, prioritize and take on the work you have to do, for the sake of your effectiveness and well-being.** As you go through this section, keep in mind the realities of your own particular situation.

We've all seen a myriad of "to-do list" systems. Today there are many computer-based organizational apps and smartphone-based apps. And there are some low-tech ways that don't require any app—not much more than having a written to-do list and crossing things off when they're done. For me personally, the simpler the better (see below). Whatever the method, in this day and age everyone needs some way to keep track of things they need to get done or would at least like to get to accomplish eventually.

This life skill is not just for task-oriented types. In fact, those brothers and sisters will likely need less guidance. Having some sort of system or method for managing one's tasks is especially helpful for the spontaneous ones among us. The last thing we would want is to turn them into task-oriented introverts spending too much time at their desks. But whatever our strengths and weaknesses, we all need some way to keep track of our upcoming responsibilities, odd jobs, projects and deadlines. The person with a poor approach to these things will likely not be free to maximize face-to-face ministry time with people. A good system should not increase the time you spend on tasks, **but** rather economize it.

The tasks system I propose here is for your ministry life. You could employ the same tools for your tentmaking role, and you could even integrate the two. And some of you might want to try to use a system to organize in your home personal life too, but that's totally optional.

Advantages of a Good System

   1. Nothing important gets forgotten.
   Brad asks Sarah if she'll look over a paper he's written for his organization, and she says, "Sure." He tells her he needs her input by Wednesday, and she agrees. She has every intention of following through with this. But Wednesday rolls around and Brad asks her about it, and all she can say is, "Whoops. I really wanted to do that. Sorry! Is it too late?" It is, and everyone is frustrated and the paper isn't as helpful as it could have been.
   Mark's friend Sultan asks Mark if he could say a few words at his upcoming engagement party. But the time comes around and Mark hasn't given it any thought at all. So he stands up and says some disjointed things, but it fails to honor his friend like he had

aspired to. An opportunity for good witness has been lost. Obviously the solution was to jot a note down about what needs to be done, and to get to it before the party.

2. You are liberated from having to keep things in your head. The person who just tries to keep in their conscious brain the nine things they really must do this week is continually expending mental energy just doing so. It is also, to some extent, preventing them from just being fully in the moment during the day, because some percentage of their circuitry is working to keep those matters from being forgotten, even if subconsciously.

3. Tasks will be completed according to priority and with less stress. I know someone who actually likes loose ends. I won't say who, but her name is on a marriage certificate in my filing cabinet. But the older she gets, the more she realizes that approach can be counter-productive, and that there is satisfaction in finishing projects. Throughout the day we all have a tendency to default to just doing what grabs our attention, or simply where we're getting affirmation, or what is most enjoyable. Those paths of least resistance have a strong magnetic pull on us. So this is when we need to walk in the Spirit, asking God to build self-control into our lives. I'm not saying we must always first eat our spinach. On the contrary, I find that when I jump into something that at first has a hurdle or inertia to overcome (like writing!), once I get rolling on it, I find a lot of satisfaction in doing it. When we give priority to the wrong things, matters of lesser or zero importance, it might feel easier in the moment. But at the end of the week we realize that not much of value was actually accomplished. As Proverbs says, "The soul of the sluggard craves and gets nothing, while the soul of the diligent is richly supplied," (13:4) and "The sluggard does not plow in the autumn; he will seek at harvest and have nothing" (20:4). And it reminds us again of what Paul said in Ephesians 5:15-16: "Look carefully then how you walk, not as unwise but as wise, making the best use of the time, because the days are evil." As long as we remain in this lost world, we carry on in our stewardship from Jesus.

4. You'll have the tools you need to tackle large, important projects. We all know that life and ministry are not just the 47 items on your to-do list. No. Oftentimes the important work is other than discreet, individual tasks. We also need an approach that works with our bigger projects and recurring commitments. For example, let's say you're pretty fluent in your ministry language, but you want to continue to improve. How? One way would be to schedule two 2-hour blocks of time each week to make special visits where local friends will help you improve, you add to your vocabulary, you read, or you do active listening in the language (e.g. with radio call-in talk shows). See Element #4 below for more specific examples.

5. Carve out an appropriate amount of time for your individual work. All of us have things we need to tackle just by ourselves (e.g. reading, correspondence, personal planning, preparing for a meeting). We would like the amount of time we spend doing this sort of work not to be too little (which would cause necessary things to pile up) or too much (resulting in having less time for more important things). A good system can actually reduce your "admin time." For example, let's say you're weak in people skills and not gifted in evangelism. You would dearly love to spend more time with local friends and, Lord willing, have opportunity to share the good news of Christ, but somehow it doesn't happen nearly as much as you would like. As a friend of mine teaches, if you are a task-oriented person, then simply make time with local friends into a *task*. Suddenly it feels more doable and your motivation level goes up.

Elements of a Good System

Below I describe my simple manual task list system, along with a sample of a week's planning. That's good. As we've said, we're all individuals, and there is no one-size-fits-all perfect solution. So let's consider 6 elements your task management system should have—whatever it is, or whatever tool you decide to use.

1. Keep a calendar. This is how you keep track of your upcoming events. Duh! I think most of us by now use some kind of online calendar. I have Google calendar and use three colors: **pink** for regularly recurring blocks on different days (see #4 below); **green** for reminders (for credit card payment reminders, birthdays, or anything with a due date); and **blue** for things like meetings and scheduled visits. I use the top bit that covers multiple days for trips. At the beginning of each day when you're planning out your tasks, don't forget to consult your calendar! Kind of basic.

2. Capture tasks. Super important. As new things come up, you've got to have an easy way to write them down or enter them into your system. The benefit of this is that you are freed from the burden of remembering things in your head.

3. Lay out all your possible tasks or projects for the week at the beginning of each work week. This is crucial. As you can see in Figure 3 below, the possible tasks or projects for the week are in my left-hand column, and the daily lists are in the other two columns. This is an example of my week's handwritten to-do list, during a light period of time. It is a running list of things week-to-week that I hope to get to at some point, either soon or at least before Jesus returns…or maybe not. Some are new. Others have been there for a really long time. I said 'manual,' but I actually keep that list on a spreadsheet on my laptop. But the rest of it is manual. Anyway, at the beginning of every week I
a) Cross off from the list the things that got done;
b) add anything needing adding, if I haven't already; and
c) print it out
Then daily on that paper I layout the tasks of that day (#5 below).

4. Decide time blocks for recurring work. Like we just discussed above, under *Advantages*, we all have projects that we break up and work on in recurring chunks of time on different days of the week. Decide what those are for you, what days you want to do them, for how long and when. Then put them on your calendar, setting them up to repeating, daily, weekly or monthly. Here are a few practical examples of such things (not that any of us have all of these). Like I said earlier, I have such items in pink in my Google Calendar—but, of course, there's nothing magical about that.

a longer time of personal prayer
in-depth Bible study
writing projects
preparation for your times with others, including praying together, one-on-one times, group times, meetings—whether with fellow workers or with local friends
special reading blocks
homework or class preparation
research you want to do
1-2 hours each week to upgrade your evangelism tools
ongoing projects (broken down into manageable components)

What happens if something comes up and you don't get to your *pink* items that day? No worries. Don't feel like you need to cram it into the next day.

If something involves another person (e.g. prayer time with your spouse or going out to meet people with a partner), then put it in the calendar as an event, rather than as a task on your to-dos.

5. At the beginning of each day, take a minute to simply write out all the possible tasks for that day, as you can see on mine (Figure 3). You might want to include any recurring time block items, if that helps not to forget them and to give them proper priority.

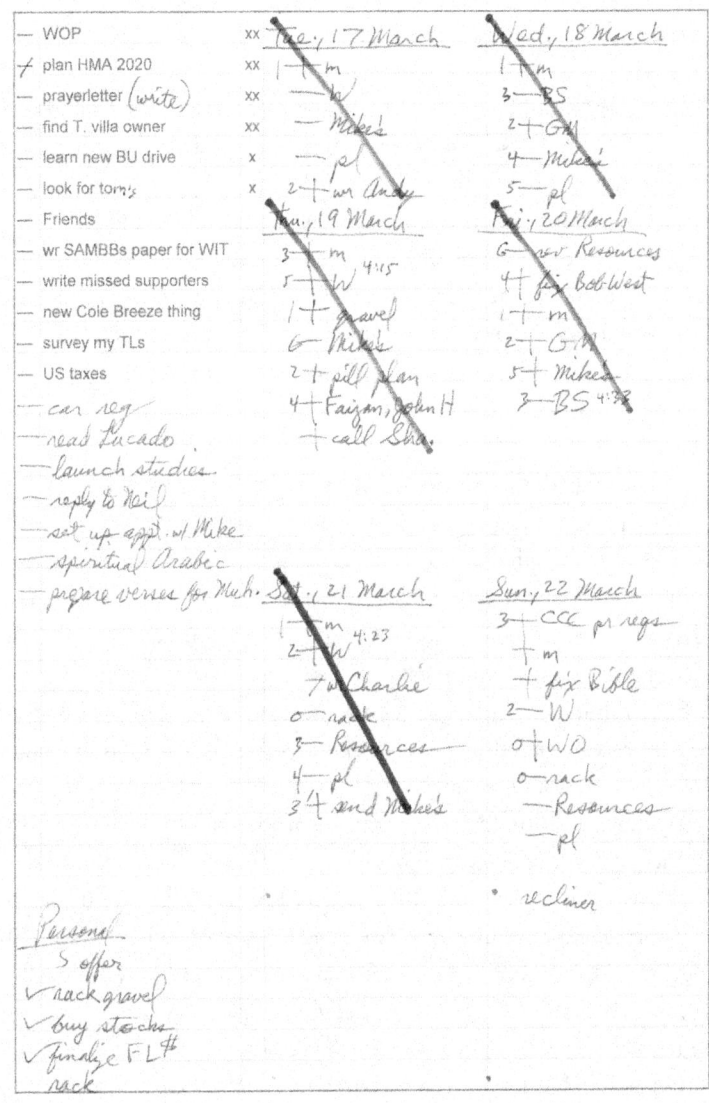

Figure 3 - Scheduling for the week

6. Finally, for that day, number them in order of priority. Most days, you won't get to everything, and that's how it should be.

What system should you use? Use mine or use something that fits you better. In any case, feel free to tailor any system to work for you. Whatever it is, it should be simple—requiring just a few minutes to set out the likely course of the week and the day. If you want to use one of the many good apps out there, just make sure it has all six of the Elements of a Good System (above). If up till now you have been working without an effective system, let today be when that changes and you get more control over the priorities the Lord has given you.

Life Skill #5: Practicing a Regular Sabbath

One of God's great gifts to the Jewish people is his commandment to "remember the Sabbath day, to keep it holy."[22] Patterned after God's **working** of Creation for six days and then His *rest* on the seventh, Israel was to work for six days and to rest on the seventh. It was the fourth of the Ten Commandments.[23] It was indeed a "day off," a day of rest. But more than that it was intended to be a special day blessed by God and made holy among the Jewish nation. When they observed the rest and holiness of the day, they benefitted in many ways—spiritually, physically, emotionally, in the family, and in social health and cohesion. A "Sabbath day's journey"[24] was not a good long hike, but rather the opposite. It was the limited short distance you could walk on a Sabbath without violating rabbinic law [2,000 cubits, or less than a half mile]. Isaiah 58:13 associates the Sabbath with pleasure, delight and success; and Hosea 2:11 with mirth and feasting. Sounds like fun actually. Other passages allude to spiritual activity, at least on some Sabbaths, such as prayer, meditation, and hearing of the law. It was and is, of course, Saturday.[25]

Even today in many societies, people work seven days a week, or make their employees do so. Some do so by choice and others without having a choice. In the country in which we live, that is technically illegal, but in reality, many employees have no alternative if they want to keep their jobs. Though for most of human history working seven days a week might have been the norm, in modern times to do so for months on end rightly feels as such a tyranny. Put that way, we can appreciate the great gift God was giving Israel as they moved out of the slavery of Egypt.

Creation was crafted by God with a cycle of 7 in view. Not only is the number 7 of importance to our bodies and psyches, some point out that it's also prominent in biology (e.g. 7 vertebrae, 7 layers of skin), physics (e.g. a cycle of 7 in the ocean waves), and possibly even economics[26] and of course 7 games in baseball's World Series!

What Does the New Testament Teach?

Whether or not Christians are to observe the Sabbath, or to observe Sunday in a similar way, has been debated over the centuries. The "Lord's day" (Acts 20:7; 1 Corinthians 16:2; Revelation 1:10) was doubtless Sunday, honoring the day of His resurrection. Keeping of the Sabbath is the only one of the Ten Commandments NOT repeated for Christ-followers in the New Testament. Holding Christian meetings on Sundays was the Early Church practice, but it was not a commandment. Hence, many Christian or denominational traditions hold great flexibility on this point. The evidence would say that the New Testament doesn't teach that Jesus-followers must strictly keep Saturday or Sunday as a holy day off. Therefore to not do so is not a sin, and it is not a sin to not hold to a Sabbath day of some sort.

Four Reasons to Practice a Sabbath or Weekly Day Off

Now permit me to sound contradictory. Paul says, "'All things are lawful,' but not all things are helpful. 'All things are lawful,' but not all things build up." (1 Corinthians 6:12 and 10:23). If I work at my tentmaking and ministry seven days a week, it's not necessarily sin. **But I am convinced that it is unwise and unhealthy.** In fact, to do so over an extended period of time is quite unwise. I'm convinced that **Gospel workers need a regular Sabbath or day-off**. I'm now using the two terms interchangeably. This will have a profound impact on your life.

Why do we need a regular day-off, even though most of us are Gentiles and not under the Mosaic Law? Here are four great reasons to take a Sabbath:

1. Our brains are wired to need it. The Jewish people have millennia of more or less observing the Sabbath and have clearly benefitted.[27] While the Lord did not choose to extend the Fourth Commandment to all the earth,[28] there is the one-in-seven principle that all would be wise to honor. Just as agricultural land needs fallow time off,[29] so too the mind and body need a fallow one-day-in-seven to rest, recharge, remember, rejuvenate, revitalize, revive, renew, regenerate, restore, refresh, and any other re- ("again") words you can recall. Clearly God created our physiology and psychology as cyclical. As Dr. Curt Thompson points out, "Neuroscience research has discovered that people with a reasonable balance and level of helpful integrated communication between the different areas of their brains tend to have reduced anxiety and a greater sense of well-being."[30] I don't see how that can happen if we're constantly driving mainly one part of our brain 24/7. Burnout is responsible for 20% of all pastoral resignations. As David Murray points out, "Every victim of burnout will tell you that unhealthy patterns of living and working that they learned in their youth caused their downfall later in life."[31] Those who work seven days a week crave some time off, so they can catch their breath. But they can't because of how they have structured their life.

2. Overwork takes a toll. We don't need a professional counselor to tell us that overwork—workaholism—can destroy our marriage and family life. This is not a book about anxiety, depression, burnout, suicide, divorce or ruined relationships with one's children. But no one can doubt how we cross the line into those territories if there is a chronic lack of rest and cultivating quality relationships with your family.

Just as an aside, the reader may be aware that in recent years anxiety, depression and suicides have skyrocketed in the U.S. and

other countries. Here are a few books I would highly recommend as very relevant:
Reset: Living a Grace-Paced Life in a Burnout Culture by David Murray;
Leading on Empty: Refilling Your Tank and Renewing Your Passion by Wayne Cordeiro;
Anxious for Nothing: Finding Calm in a Chaotic World by Max Lucado;
Enjoy Life: Healing with Happiness by Lynn Johnson.
When our three kids were all young, we lived in Jordan. My business and ministry were both very demanding. Many evenings I was not around. But Liz made it clear: "We can still make this work so long as we can all be together one whole day each week." So Fridays were very chill. I often would get up with the kids so that Liz could sleep in. Sometimes she would even go out to breakfast—BY HERSELF. We were part of a co-ed softball league. The kids loved watching their parents embarrass themselves on the field, while hanging out with their friends on the wall. After the game our family would go out for burgers and ice cream. They still mention those times as some of their richest childhood memories.

3. More work is not better. If we're working 40 hours a week, we naturally assume that if we work 60 hours a week, we'll get 50% more done. Wrong! There are a gazillion studies that show how at some point staying at the grindstone for longer hours does **not** enable us to achieve more. For example, the research of Dr. John Pencavel, economics professor at Stanford University, would indicate that work after 50 or 55 hours per week is basically pointless.[32]

4. Overwork is a spiritual problem. To chronically overwork is to tell God that you don't need Him or trust Him to work through your ministry. Yikes. None of us would ever articulate that to the Lord, but that is sometimes exactly what we are thinking—if we are thinking. How many on the field have become

ministry-holics? The nature of our work can seem so perpetually uncompleted. When there's little fruit, we re-triple our efforts. Or conversely, when the ministry really starts to take off and there's more to do, we throw ourselves into it without regard for margins. It's easy to slip into the mode of going at all hours, not realizing that it's mostly driven by adrenaline and possibly ego. Either way, we're not getting the rest we need and we are violating the principles of Psalm 127:

Unless the LORD builds the house, those who build it labor in vain. Unless the LORD watches over the city, the watchman stays awake in vain.
² It is in vain that you rise up early and go late to rest, eating the bread of anxious toil; for he gives to his beloved sleep.
³ Behold, children are a heritage from the LORD, the fruit of the womb a reward.
⁴ Like arrows in the hand of a warrior are the children of one's youth.
⁵ Blessed is the man who fills his quiver with them! He shall not be put to shame when he speaks with his enemies in the gate.

This is so full of profound insights. It touches on virtually every practical aspect of life, all the things we seek after. Its main point is not that we need God to build a house. People all over the world build nice houses without a relationship with God. Rather, the psalmist is saying that the believer has a choice to make in his or her daily life: We can either tirelessly work **as if it all depends on ourselves**, overdoing it and not breaking off at a decent time—"eating the bread of anxious toil." Or we can trust Yahweh to bless and provide and enrich in His way for us, because it **ultimately all depends on Him** and not on ourselves. In fact, He wants to work for us "even in [our] sleep"—the likely meaning of the Hebrew of verse 2b. This psalm is about faith, about going through life with a calm reliance on Him rather than on self. Always going at it with the mindset that it really depends on me rather than on Him eventually degrades life.

So, taking a Sabbath day-off is a powerful demonstration of faith.

Have you ever taken stock of the good and valuable parts of your life? I did that once and came up with something like this:

- My walk with God
- My wife and marriage
- My kids
- A satisfying ministry that fits our gifts and calling, and by the grace of God seems valuable for the Kingdom
- Our general health
- Many wonderful friendships
- The respect of our peers
- God's steady provision financially (and thankfulness for all our financial and prayer partners)

Don't get me wrong. Our lives are far from circumstantially perfect. But it occurred to me how the most valuable aspects were definitely not attributable to my cleverness and vigilance but were from God's Psalm 127 blessing and work for me.

Finally, Some Practical Tips for Taking a Sabbath

• **Find a good time.** If you're married, the two of you should sit down, pray and decide on which day of the week will work best. Don't be frustrated if none of the seven are **perfect**. Expect tradeoffs. God knows. If your tentmaking could allow for it, even consider a day in the middle of the week, as weekends may be best for visits or team functions.

• **Be consistent.** While on some days off things will come up, and some ministry matters might occasionally be unavoidable, try to make the time fully OFF as consistent as possible. Don't let yourself slip into any ministry or tentmaking tasks. Liz and I don't see people we don't want to see, and often we didn't answer the phone. No "shoulds" allowed (e.g. I should write that email. I should paint the guestroom. I should prepare for tomorrow morning's meeting.). I often get a thought, "Oh, I need to do such-and-such real quick so I don't forget." But if it feels like a "should," it's a task for tomorrow and not for today.

- **Fill it with pleasant things.** Remember all those Old Testament verses about holy rest? Someone has suggested that Sabbaths are for us to ***pray, play and rest***. That seems a good reflection of the Scriptural passages. One feature I really like about our days off is that I give myself permission to eat whatever I want. I'm not sure why that's not in Deuteronomy. Probably a copyist's error. The biblical Sabbath is NOT like a sort of Puritanism that H. L. Mencken makes fun of as "The haunting fear that someone, somewhere, may be happy."[33] ☺

- **Make it personal.** What is life-giving for you? Some like to completely unplug for the whole day. That seems wise, but you need to figure out what best ministers to your spirit. I actually enjoy relaxing by looking at interesting online articles, reading my Kindle or watching TV. But I've learned that even glancing at my email inbox can spoil my mood. Many love going on walks out in nature, if that's possible in your situation.

- **It takes practice to rest**. Don't be surprised if initially for a few hours your brain is missing those dopamine injections! That's actually a good sign, a sign that you are winding down.

- **Remember your goal.** Don't worry if your day-off is not always super fun. The key marker is not how good of a time you had on your day off, but what were the restorative effects on your soul.

- **Make a day of it.** Some workers tell me that they have a whole Sabbath each week—just not all at the same time. They might break it up, taking off Friday morning plus Sunday afternoon plus Wednesday evening. I really don't see how that matches the biblical expectations of Sabbath or is meeting our mental and emotional needs. There is something about taking a whole day, usually because it takes us about half the day to actually mentally get into a place of rest. The beauty of a Sabbath is waking up on a morning, knowing that no work or burden is required of us that day. Then the mind can wind down like it needs to.

This doesn't mean you can't see teammates or others on your Sabbath. Only that it should just be for enjoying the relationship without an agenda.

May the Lord give you wisdom and grace as you explore His will for your life in this very vital area. *Shabbat shalom*!

Life Skill #6: Finding a Suitable Tentmaking Situation[34]

A few years ago I was visiting with a family in one of the six Arab Gulf countries.[35] Let me describe the husband's tentmaking job: It was in his professional field and paid very well. His work hours were a steady 35 hours a week (somewhat typical for that country), which left him time for ministry at work and outside of work as well. Most of the time on the job he was with locals, and there were often times for spiritual and personal conversations. And many of the interactions were in Gulf Arabic, so this was good for his ever-improving language.

I've also visited friends whose job were less than a blessing. I recently asked one single woman how her tentmaking was. She was a schoolteacher, and she said it was OK. So I asked her how much she had to work at the job. She said it only took 50-60 hours a week; but if you included grading papers at home it was more like 80-90 hours! That same week I met a brother who had just quit his school teaching situation, as he shared how it had been a miserable two years. He faced long hours, total chaos in the classroom, and no support from the administration. He was in the process of making a radical shift in his residency and tentmaking, as his job literally prevented him from pursuing the purposes why God brought them there. Some do like their teaching jobs, but those roles do seem to consistently carry special challenges.

As I previously mentioned, I used to have my own small business in Jordan. This put me in contact with business leaders. And the office was a good place for Bible studies with believers and others. I've seen others whose businesses swallowed them alive, lost six figures of dollars, and eventually failed.

The tentmaking environment varies considerably from country-to-country. For example, most gospel workers in the Gulf have good jobs and make good money. But flexibility can be a problem. A few in the Gulf have sort of general visas, and the burdens on their time and energies are much less demanding. In other parts of the 10/40 Window it's easier to get residency, have part-time jobs, or launch a small business or NGO. Often in those countries the economy and business environment are weak and actually making a decent profit is rare. In those contexts, sometimes *viability* is more of a challenge.

Some workers truly want a fulltime job or business or NGO. Others really do not, in order to leave lots of time for ministry outside the workplace. I've often seen this correlation: If the person back home was an engineer, schoolteacher, or businessperson, then they're more likely to prefer a fulltime professional role on the field. If the person back home was in vocational ministry, then most prefer to maximize their time outside their tentmaking. But that, of course, is not 100%.

A friend of mine told me of his current situation:

> I am director of a branch office of a US based NGO and have a contract to manage water projects in [neighboring country] that is limited to 20 hours per week. I need to have a lot of additional financial support to offset the cost of living here but we've made it work and make sense for people we know here and there. (I call it the 50/50 model—about half my time to tentmaking and half my salary from it. The rest to CP efforts and salary from churches.)

If this picture wasn't already complicated enough, add to this the necessity of learning the language. I strongly believe in making the huge investment of time and effort toward becoming well conversational and functional in the language. Studies have shown that one's ability to connect with people in their heart language will make a huge difference in their ministry in the long run. For couples, it's important for at least one person of the couple to attain good language functionality; but it's even better if both can. Generally this takes around two years of fulltime work to attain a good foundation. When is that going to happen? Normally, there are two ways that work best: Somehow be fulltime in language work in your new country. OR Get your foundations in the language in another country in the region, where fulltime language learning is possible. To arrive in your target country without the language and with a fulltime job almost never leads to language proficiency. Many teams will not accept such a person onto the team.

The bottom-line is this: There is likely no other aspect of your life on the field that will have a greater impact on your time than your tentmaking situation. Therefore it behooves you to really pray through this area, as a couple if married, and seek God's leading and provision. Think through what your ideal situation might look like. What are your connections, marketable skills, etc.? Talk to lots of people in-country as to what opportunities seem to be available and make quality plans and lay the groundwork in advance. Don't worry if you don't get your ideal at first. Nothing has to be set in stone over the years. **If your present tentmaking situation is not good, then really consider changing it**. Pray to the Lord of the Harvest for creative alternatives.

Types of residency situations in most countries:

1. Having a job. This encompasses a huge variety.
2. Having a business (or being a partner in such). Again, there's a wide spectrum. This can include business in services, goods, or trade, either working on your own, with a partner, or with many employees.
3. Running an NGO/humanitarian project.
4. Studying as a grad student.
5. Having *no* job or business. "Other." There are sometimes general kinds of visas, sponsors, the possibility of being on a tourist visa for an extended period, business exploratory visas, church visas, opening a trade company and not feeling pressured to be fulltime at it, and such. In some countries, investor visas, retirement visas, and freelance visas may also give you a great deal of time flexibility.

Seven facets of tentmaking (generally)

All of these five types have pros and cons. What aspects of tentmaking are important to you? Here are things to consider as you make your decisions. No situation achieves them all; you might just achieve 3 or 4 of these:

1. Residency (visa). I still remember the pride I felt when I received my first plasticized ID card in Jordan with my picture on it. I belonged. I was legit. No more fuzzy status.
2. Identity. Some call this viability. In other words, your role in society makes perfect sense to people. Ironically, some situations give residency without good viability; and some give excellent identity but fail for some reason to give legal residency, i.e. what you do is clear and solid, but you may need to be a on a tourist visa for a while.
3. Flexibility and a low time requirement of the tentmaking role. As described, this is very important for some people. Maximize your time outside the job for pursuing relationships, doing media follow up, improving your language, running a team, discipling believers, teaching the Word, developing gospel explanations or apologetics, mentoring other workers, apostolically guiding a **Disciple Making Movement** (see Chapter 4), and so on. Those with highly demanding jobs usually don't get to do a lot of that.
4. Access. It puts you around the people you are endeavoring to reach for Christ, either work colleagues, clients, suppliers or employees. This is not to be taken for granted. Unfortunately, in some countries where local citizens are in the minority, your job might have you with everybody EXCEPT locals.
5. Serving the poor and needy in practical ways. This often means an NGO. But sometimes a for-profit business can accomplish this better, e.g. by providing many jobs.
6. Income. Do you hate the idea of raising support? Would you rather be waterboarded than bring up financial needs to potential donors? Then get a job with a good salary! But even if you have a high-paying job, you'll still want to make sure you

have solid support from home. A friend of mine in Saudi Arabia advises an 80/20 Rule: Don't have more than 80% of your total needs met by your job, as that would rob you the blessing of having partners with you from back home and their committed prayer support. And don't have less than 20% be from your local income, as that wouldn't be optically viable. Makes sense.
7. Language and culture learning. Again, some situations provide an excellent context for this while others do not.

Some have said that if you do not have a fulltime job, then you are a "job faker." I personally don't buy that. Of course, we must not be dishonest, for example saying that you run a consulting business, but that last time you did any consulting work was 3 years ago. Whatever we tell people we do, we should do. However, it is perfectly OK to be far less than fulltime at it time-wise. And no one's going to see your paystubs.

Increasingly there are more and more creative set-ups or solutions for our role and residency in society. Typically in the past it was the husband who would have the visa-obtaining job or business, however now in some families it is the wife who has that, and this is not considered strange in many cultures nowadays. There are other ways to be *nimble* in your tent-making approach. For example, some are now doing **tele-tentmaking**. [Have I coined a new missions term?] Some teach English online, and some are physicians practicing tele-medicine with patients around the world, and some are software developers or web designers with clients in other continents. It's all real and gives you a good viable explanation for what you do. Some friends of mine obtained their residency one way but ended up doing other professional activities. With the visa in-hand, they have flexibility to pursue what works out best. One bought a trading company. He worked at that a bit, but nothing worked out very well. Then he worked on his PhD for a few years, and obtained it, and now teaches at a university part-time. He's still on the trading company visa, even though it has never really taken off like he had hoped. All of it has been real and honest. Generally Immigration departments aren't going to split hairs as long as they see the person contributing to society.

Making it personal

So what are the priorities for YOU? How is the Lord leading in your life and calling? If you are a doctor or nurse and plan to simply carry on doing the same in your intended country on the field, then this is an easy, simple issue for you. If you got your master's degree or certificate in being a professional teacher of English as a second language, then again, problem solved. Others might take one of their hobbies and turn it into a small business. For example, a friend is an avid racing cyclist and has a business in Southeast Asia making custom-designed super-light alloy frames. But for any of us, let's not let the tail wag the dog. Our vision for how we think the Lord can use us on the field should guide our tentmaking direction and not the other way around. We remember that the Apostle Paul was highly educated in law, and yet that profession would not have served his calling. So to provide for himself and others in itinerant ministry, he would commercially **make tents**—the manual trade he had also learned as a youth (as Jewish theological students were required to learn a trade). It was lucrative, but it gave him the flexibility to energetically go after the ministry in various cities to which Jesus had called him. Many among us will carry on with our profession in our field life. And others, like myself, will let go of that specific career for something else more conducive. (My degree and previous employment in the US was in computer engineering, information technology.) Don't be discouraged. It is not unusual for it to take up to 4 years before a person settles into a role that feels best for them. May the Lord give you wisdom in this important part of the adventure!

Life Skill #7: More Hacks to Free Up Your Schedule

By now you have figured out that there are ways for you to get more positive control over your time and schedule. There are ways to reduce the overall load, to bring more balance into your life and help you focus on what really counts. These include working resourcefully with your e-communications, having a really good task management system that works for you, protecting your Sabbath days, and prayerfully evaluating your tentmaking situation. And it also includes NOT taking shortcuts with your Quiet Times—keeping your regular time with the Lord vital. I'm often asked, "Are there ways to free up even more time?" Usually a question like this arises from the crippling feeling that he or she isn't getting enough time in something they consider really important. It can also come from someone who is nearing burnout from an unsustainable schedule. Be encouraged! The answer for most people is 'yes.' I'll never forget the time we had George Verwer, founder of Operation Mobilization, speak at our big conference. "I have a message from God for all your team leaders." Then he shouted, "Cut. Cut. Cut!" Here are 11 more ways to do just that:

1. **Reduce your hours in your tentmaking job.** This might seem to you as quite doable, or may seem to you as impossible. In fact it might be achievable. As author Chester Karrass has said: "You don't get what you deserve. You get what you negotiate." A friend of mine is a highly qualified physician. When she and her family were moving to the Gulf, she knew that medical jobs were very demanding, but that she really needed a part-time job (though with visa and benefits). At first it was *impossible*. ("There's absolutely no way we can make a contract like that.") Then it seemed *difficult*. ("OK, we can promise to hold down your hours to 40 a week."). Then *done*. She now works a consistent 2/3 schedule, which is just right. A lot of prayer went into these negotiations, and she was persistent. Is it time to renegotiate your job?

2. If you are personally very busy running a business or NGO, **consider hiring one or two top-level people.** As the owner of my business in Jordan, the government didn't give a fig about how many hours I worked. In retrospect I wish I had taken on a local employee for marketing our services. This could have even been on commission. As the business expanded, I could have pulled out even more by hiring a trustworthy general manager. Why didn't I do that? I don't really know… I could have used a coach (see #11 below). What about you?

3. Those of you who lead a team, have you **carefully evaluated all your team functions**? When I served as Field Director I saw a wide spectrum in how much time teams spend together—and indeed there is no one-size-fits-all. Some would meet several hours a week, even multiple times per week. Other teams would have team meetings only once a month. I certainly would not recommend less than that. As mentioned, I do recommend that every field worker be committed to a *weekly prayer meeting*. This could be a team thing, or it might be more of a random group of workers from different organizations. Apart from that, teams could get by with having team meetings only every other week, every third week or even once a month. These could be for Bible study together, decisions, updates, strategy or problem-solving and general reconnecting. On top of this, some teams have weekly team social times. Again, you have to assess if that is profitable or not. It's also healthy for everyone to have good relationships outside the team and that might be meeting many social needs. Is the time your team spends together too little or too much, or is it, in the words of the storybook character Goldilocks, just right?

4. Evaluate time spent in other meetings. Besides team meetings, what about other things? In our country, there are two or three networks that are inter-agency or non-organization based. They each have gatherings at a regional level, country level, and even city level. A worker, especially a team leader, could fill up their calendar with meetings like this, all giving the illusion of progress, though sometimes the networking is worthwhile. Nonetheless, most of us need to take a scalpel to these in our schedule. We can't do everything. Can we ruthlessly evaluate what really helps us in our calling and effectiveness? Am I making a Kingdom contribution to those networks, where I believe the Lord would have me continue to say 'yes' or not? Sometimes the answer may not be to stop going, but maybe to press for shorter, less frequent, or online meetings.

5. Learn to say "no." For some of us, this is a biggie. There is no shortage of requests and most of us simply can't do all that is asked of us. We can't go to every meeting, join every project or committee we're invited to, say yes to favors asked of us, or even open our doors in hospitality every time there's a need. So we need to learn to graciously say "no" to many things. A friend once confided in me that this is not only the number one frustration in his time stewardship, but also in his marriage. So we worked through many real life examples of things that had come up in the past six months. He could see in hindsight that he could say yes to some things but should have said no to other things. There was an example when he had said yes to a brother but knew he should have declined. So I asked, "If you could rewind, how would you have handled it differently?" That was helpful to think through. For him, though, saying no is an emotional struggle. He feels terrible when he does so, and that's why he doesn't do it nearly enough. So we put together a 3-step process: a) Evaluate if you should do it or not. Involve others in the decision when necessary. Don't feel you need to give an answer on the spot. Sometimes just saying, "Let me talk it over with my family" or "with my overseer" gives you the time you need. b) If the right response is to say no, think through a gracious way to decline. For example, you could even explain why the Lord would not have you take it on or help at this time. Or you can suggest other people or alternatives. Or blame it on this book, lol. c) Move on and don't feel guilty about it. Remember this: For everything you say yes to, you are automatically saying no to something else (e.g. time with your kids, or a strategic project that you keep putting off).

6. Delegate! No doubt there are things you are doing that someone else could do. Your spouse, your kids, friends, others on the team, or an employee. A good friend Nick was moving to Egypt with a large team and was about to be met with immense academic and professional responsibilities. How could he lead a team, learn the language, and carry this big tentmaking role? Answer: He couldn't; it was impossible. So as a team they broke down all the bits that team leaders normally do, and then they delegated virtually ALL of them to individual members. They would maintain social links, but only meet all together once a month. Not only did this free up Nick enormously, but it instantly made everyone on team more of a **stakeholder**. It was impressive. Another friend, Carlos, told me that he used to feel that he could comfortably delegate out a task only if the person taking it on could do 80% as well or better compared with how he would do it. Later he became so swamped, he said the threshold was now 50%! Today what should you drop?

7. Keep alert for time-wasters. They're out there. What are they? First of all, I'm not necessarily talking about things you like to do, time with family and friends, activities that help you rest or refresh. Rather we're talking about things we do somewhat regularly, but which upon reflection may not be worth it. The cost outweighs the benefit. Let's take Facebook as an example. You have a growing number of Facebook friends, and you enjoy keeping up with them, and catching up with friends from many years ago. Sometimes the serious posts are stimulating and the funny bits amusing. It now takes more time to go through posts and private messages. What used to be a 10-minute fun break has now morphed into a 45-minute daily duty, because if you don't 'like' all your friends' posts, some will assume that you are mad at them. Now it seems more like a waste of time. The same thing can happen with almost any escape, be it TV watching, hiking, reading novels, or keeping up with all your emails and e-messages. I'm not saying stop doing all of these things. But you do want to keep an eye on these things and cut back on whatever isn't giving you the benefit you should be getting from it. Can you think of one example of something that has become a time-waster in your life right now?

8. Find ways to **do more online**. One positive outcome of the coronavirus calamity of 2020 is that we learned we could do a lot more online than we previously thought possible. Evaluate: What

am I doing in-person or manually (e.g. physical meetings, commuting, paperwork, etc.) that could be done more efficiently online?

9. Consider dropping something MAJOR. Are you presently swamped? Living and working in the **red zone** far too long? As an illustration, cars with manual transmission will show revolutions per minute. When the car is revved up too much, and the RPMs are too high, the needle will go into the red zone of the gauge. That is fine momentarily but will burn out the transmission if you stay there too long. If this is reflective of how you feel, this is probably a sign that there is something on your plate that should be taken off or perhaps just postponed a year or more. Examples might be a degree program you're in, an expansion phase in your business, rebuilding a car as a hobby, taking on the leadership of something you should actually get out of, driving the kids 3 hours twice a week for soccer practice, joining your organization's executive committee, and so on. There ARE enough hours in the day to carry out what the Lord wants you to do, but maybe not everything your eyes desire. I'll say it again: People tend to overestimate what they can accomplish in the short-term and underestimate what they can do in the long-term. Be sensible for the now. Is there something major you should drop?

10. Spend money to multiply your time. All over the world gospel workers have found tremendous relief in time and energy by hiring a nanny for the younger kids, a cook, or a cleaning person Some amongst us are reluctant to do so, as they are not used to it in their home country, they don't want to appear rich, and they don't want to have to write home about it. It's okay. Often the context on the field is very different. In Jordan, sometimes even the maids had maids. The priority here is you being more effective and productive. Others hire a language helper who will come to your home, a tutor to help your kids with their math, or a driver (remember the kids' soccer practices?). When there are legal matters or complicated processes with government departments, don't try to figure it all out yourself and do it yourself—standing in endless lines. Hire a lawyer or expediter who does this stuff for a living, and who has the connections you do not have. Do you enjoy painting and decorating and have the time? Then sure, paint those bedrooms yourself. Otherwise, hire it out. What takes up time in your life right now that doesn't really have to, if you were to spend a few bucks? Imagine Ryan and Melanie arriving on the field with a 4-year old and a toddler. They both intend to learn the language well and have loads of relationships with locals. They're both intrinsically motivated and eager to hit the ground running. Is there any possible way they could BOTH be fulltime in those pursuits (assuming no tentmaking)? If they have a live-in nanny/cook/cleaner, plus utilizing some daycare, they might get close to that objective. After a year and a half or so they will be well on their way.

11. And last but not least, **get a coach.** Successful companies all over the world have discovered that hiring life coaches for their top executives is well worth whatever it costs. These coaches meet once a week one-on-one with their clients for around an hour and discuss whatever might be frustrating in the person's life —and not just professional, company matters. It might be tactical hurdles or big life issues. Usually they talk out the particular subject, working through a process of **guided self-discovery** to bring solutions, not just telling them what to do. You can't afford the $250/hour cost for this? Is there a friend or leader or mentor in your life who could serve you this way, either where you live or someone back home? All of us could be more fruitful and more centered than we are, and this could be a way to get there. Who is someone you admire who you could ask to be a coach or mentor to you?

We've now covered seven Life Skills related to healthy time stewardship, with lots of specifics. So how can you know if you're doing well or doing poorly? What can give you the unvarnished picture and tell you the areas where change is needed? And if so, what sort of change? Finally, let's now let **the rubber meet the road by developing a time budget**.

Life Skill #8: Making a "Time Budget"

Becky has a good steady job, but not a huge income. Living on her own, the expenses pile up: rent, utilities, car payment, insurance and maintenance, internet and phone, groceries and so forth. She also wants to give some to the Lord's work, to take some vacation time every year, and even to save a bit. To avoid running up her credit card balance, she is keen to see how she can live within her means. There's not much she can do about her level of income, short of winning the lottery. But she senses there might be some flexibility regarding her expenses. So she asks a friend who's good with finances and numbers to help her develop a budget. As a result, she sees that overall it works—barely—and she decides to make some strategic adjustments: changing to a more modest used car, not going to Starbucks every day, and cooking for herself more. She'll make wiser use of heat in the winter and AC in the summer. She's now in the driver's seat of her money because of having a financial budget. As the months progress, she will be able to see if her expenditures in the different categories are what she has been aiming for, and make further adjustments as necessary.

Just as it's essential and helpful to make a financial budget, so it is to make a **time budget**. This exercise will only take an hour or so, and hopefully it is already clear why this has lots of potential to help you. By now you've accumulated some really good ideas, some paradigm shifts in principles, a couple of new methods, and buckets of wonderful intentions. But in the months ahead, where will your time **actually** go? You can't manage what you can't measure. Creating a time budget should bring clarity beyond what you thought possible. Lord willing, this is where you proactively take control.

Over the years, I've trained many field workers in this, including preparing team leaders to help their team members develop their own time budgets. The idea is simple: envision the week, and what categories your time goes into in your ministry life, including any tentmaking. It is NOT pertaining to the **personal** sphere of your life, a la Life Skill #1 above. It should be about a **typical full week**, not one where there is vacation time, holidays, sick time off, or where you might be out of town at a conference. Again, a typical full normal week in the city in which you live. You could start by analyzing what has been in the recent past, as you can begin with a look in the rearview mirror. Or you may want to just begin with what you hope for in moving forward from today. You will gain two things through this exercise: a time budget, and a way to monitor things moving forward. Of course, it's important to pray throughout the process.

In reality, will things vary week to week? Of course they will. So you will identify your main time categories, and the typical or average hours per week in each category—for a full or normal week. The examples I give here will be about someone who is able to be fulltime in ministry, including tentmaking. But I realize that not everyone will be in fulltime mode in those spheres, such as husbands and wives who split up the available ministry time and also the domestic responsibilities, or mothers of young children who intend to major on family and home.[36]

Jason's Time Budget (final product)

After the process described below, Jason's time budget will look like this:

Jason's Time Budget	
Activity	Hours
Redemptive relationships, evangelism	6
Discipling Farid, a believer	2
His job	25
Team activities	3
Further language-learning work	3
Weekly prayer meeting	3
In-depth Bible study	2
Other	4
TOTAL	**48**

Figure 4 - Jason's final time budget

Have a look at those **endnotes** if you would like clarification on what is meant by those categories.[37]

Forty-eight hours a week might seem to you as too little or as too much. It's perhaps similar to an elder back home who has a normal job and is also active in lay ministry.

Notice that it does not include Jason's Quiet Times, but does include 2 hours a week in in-depth Bible study. This is because we consider his Quiet Times as extremely vital, and falling more into the sphere of his personal life; whereas the special times in study and prayer meetings might be best considered as part of his vocation as a gospel worker. But how you want to split the hairs is up to you.

Where to begin? How did Jason arrive at this specific framework? While you could do this just on your own, it will be better if you can have someone with you, if possible, helping you think things through step-by-step. He or she needn't be a time management guru. They could be a spouse, a team leader, a colleague or a friend. They merely need to ask questions and make sure important bits don't get forgotten, and in general to help you keep things realistic.

Step 1: Identify Your Major Categories of Work

These should probably be 5-8 categories of activity, areas of work that you pretty consistently invest in. Here is what Jason initially came up with:

- Time with local friends
- Time spent intentionally meeting new people
- Discipling Farid, a believer
- Job: teaching
- Job: admin and grading papers
- Team meetings
- Team other
- Other responsibilities from his organization
- Further language-learning work
- Weekly prayer meeting
- In-depth Bible study alone

- In-depth Bible study in my small group
- General admin stuff
- Communications with financial and prayer partners
- Dealing with our residency
- Miscellaneous

As they discussed it, Jason's friend helped him realize that was too detailed to be helpful, and that Jason should merge some of these together. He was able to simplify it from 15 categories down to a much more manageable 8.

Step 2: What is the right total per week?

Decide what is an appropriate number for **total** work/ministry-related hours per week. This is not hours in each category. That's the next step. In Step 2 simply ask yourself: "In an ideal world, how many hours a week should I be putting into my calling of this ministry here on the field (including any tentmaking)?" If one is married, this is a big picture number that should be discussed with one's spouse.

Full of zeal for the Lord, Jason at first aspired to generally work 65 hours a week. But then his wife, Becca, reminded him that he was married, had 3 kids, and that she often needed Jason to watch the kids so she too could cultivate relationships with her local friends. Therefore, being neither Superman nor Assistant Messiah, he had to be more realistic. After prayer and some difficult discussions, they reached a consensus on 48 hours a week for him.

Step 3: Estimate the number of hours for each category

Just write down the first thing that comes in your head. Even at this stage, you are beginning to reflect your priorities. Here was Jason's after his first **pass**:

Jason's Time Budget (first draft)	
Activity	Hours
Redemptive relationships, evangelism	10
Discipling Farid, a believer	4
His job	30
Team activities	6
Further language-learning work	4
Weekly prayer meeting	1
In-depth Bible study	1
Other	6
TOTAL	**62**

Figure 5 - Rough draft of Jason's time budget

Is this a problem that the numbers didn't fit? Not at all. This was just an initial first pass, a rough draft. Prayerful, thoughtful tweaking now happens in Step 4.

Step 4: Make strategic changes

The wise 2nd century Roman emperor Marcus Aurelius nailed it:

> It is essential for you to remember that the attention you give to any action should be in due proportion to its worth, for then you won't tire and give up, if you aren't busying yourself with lesser things beyond what should be allowed. Since the vast majority of our words and actions are unnecessary, corralling them will create an abundance of leisure and tranquility. As a result, we shouldn't forget at each moment to ask, is this one of the unnecessary things?[38]

Jason has 48 hours to "spend" and he has 62 hours of things to do. Problem? He now must go through again all the categories and estimates of hours per week in each, making strategic changes. Pray, mull things over, discuss details. What is too low and needs to be increased, to reflect my real priorities? What is too high and needs to somehow be pared down? This will be your 2nd Draft.

Step 5: Discuss it all with significant others.

If you haven't already, run it all by your spouse, a ministry partner, and/or team leader. Make adjustments as necessary. After doing this, that will be your third draft or final time budget.

Tracking How This Works Out Over Time

Now Jason is thinking that this is how he believes things will work out with his time, how it should work out. It's more or less consistent with his commitments and priorities. If he keeps to this more or less over time, he can feel good about his time stewardship. But how will he know if in reality it's working out as the weeks and months go by? So he decides to actually track his time over some weeks in some detail—not for weeks on end—but for two or three weeks, sort of to create a snapshot of a typical week. Here's how you can do this. It can be a little detailed-ish, so I'm going to insert here that this is **optional**, and not necessarily an essential step of making your time budget.

Jason made a simple form for himself that he could fill in (see Figure 6 at the end of chapter). He did not write things down throughout the day. That would be too tedious and distracting. Rather he took just a few minutes at the end of each day to write down best estimates. That was good enough.

I have done this for myself a few times (again, just a 2-3 week snapshot). Years ago in Jordan I asked Barney, a teammate, to do this for himself for a couple weeks after we had worked out his time budget. He agreed, and after two weeks gave me two week-grids similar to Figure 4. I said, "Well done!" and thanked him profusely. I asked if the exercise was helpful, he answered that it really was and that he wanted to continue. When I assured him that it really wasn't necessary, he insisted. So I wound up with 3 years' worth of Barney's week-grids in my filing cabinet!

I would very much recommend that you pull these 8 Life Skills out for review once a month for a while. Don't worry that you must somehow master all of these perfectly. God doesn't require a certain amount of achievement from us, nor expect perfection. We see over and over in Scripture that He wants our hearts and wants our faithfulness, and these 8 Life Skills can help you in that. It is my fervent prayer for your life and ministry to become all that the Lord wants them to be!

	Time Budget	SUN.	MON.	TUE.	WED.	THU.	FRI.	SAT.	Category Totals
Relationships & ev	6								
Discipling Farid	2								
Job	25								
Team activities	3								
Further language-learning work	3								
Weekly prayer meeting	3								
In-depth Bible study	2								
Other	4								
Totals	48								

Figure 6 - Jason's time accounting sheet

---

1. Friberg, Timothy, Friberg, Barbara and Miller, Neva. *Analytical Lexicon of the Greek New Testament*. Baker Publishing Group, 2000.
2. Friberg, Timothy, Friberg, Barbara and Miller, Neva. *Analytical Lexicon of the Greek New Testament*. Baker Publishing Group, 2000.
3. Forsee, A. *Albert Einstein, Theoretical Physicist*. New York: Macmillan, 1963. P. 81.
4. This comes in a letter to the family of Michele Besso, his life-long collaborator and closest friend, and was written a few days after Einstein learned of his death. Paul Mainwood, Quora.com, https://www.quora.com/?signup_answer_page=32388152
5. Tolle, Eckhart. *The Power of Now: A Guide to Spiritual Enlightenment*. New World Library, 2004.
6. Consider such Scripture as Psalm 46:10 and 131:1-2.
7. At times I will simply mention how something might affect our marriages and parenting. But I realize that many of the dearest and best colleagues among us are single, and I do not intend to slight their situations in any way. Singles are free to skip over the marriage or family life bits or read along that you might better appreciate the special challenges in marriage and parenting on the field or provide a different perspective.
8. Other organizations have accountability structures which vary from excessively onerous to dangerously non-existent.

9. There are some who feel they can get by on 5 hours sleep a night. Some are even able to, medically, somehow. But normal homo sapiens don't do well on less than 7-8 hours a night.
10. Including various bits like resting in His presence, private worship, etc.
11. An aspect of what Paul calls "self control" (Galatians 5:23).
12. Though the noun 'word' is not in the Greek, the adjective *'logikos'* is, and most commentators believe this is a reference to Scripture. *Expositors* suggests, "crave the unadulterated spiritual milk of the word."
13. There in Philippians 3:8 he has broadened his point beyond the inadequacy of a works righteousness.
14. I certainly don't advocate a legalistic approach to "daily," as if one should feel guilty if on a certain day he or she misses that time. We endeavor to have daily focused time with Him. But on some days, there are too many alligators in the swamp, and it just doesn't happen. There's tomorrow.
15. I like how John Ortberg of Menlo Church, Menlo Park, CA, describes how Israel groaning before God was a good thing. Grumbling was not.
16. I encourage people, especially those in leadership or teaching roles, to spend two blocks a week in in-depth Bible study. This is usually hours spent over time on a single passage. Or it can be topical as well.
17. Allen, David. *Getting Things Done: The Art of Stress Free Productivity*. New York: Penguin, 2001.
18. See Chapter 6, "Processing: Getting "In" to Empty," in Allen, *Getting Things Done*.
19. Or you can make it 2 minutes, or 4 minutes; but right in that range only.
20. Cloud, Henry and Townsend, John. *Boundaries: When to Say Yes, How to Say No To Take Control of Your Life*. Zondervan, 2017.
21. Newport, Cal. *Deep Work: Rules for focused success in a distracted world*. New York: Grand Central Publishing, 2016.
22. Exodus 20:8.
23. Exodus 20:1-17 and Deuteronomy 5:1-21.
24. Acts 1:12.
25. The sabbath technically begins on Friday at sunset.
26. https://www.kitco.com/commentaries/2015-08-13/-7-What-s-so-special-about-the-number-7.html.
27. https://en.wikipedia.org/wiki/Ashkenazi_Jewish_intelligence.
28. Perhaps as the gospel went out to all the world, holding Christians to a Sabbath would have been practically impossible in many Gentile societies.
29. https://www.gardeningknowhow.com/garden-how-to/soil-fertilizers/what-is-fallow-ground.htm.
30. Thompson, Curt. *Anatomy of the Soul*. Tyndale House Publishers, 2010. P. 41.
31. Murray, David. *Reset: Living a Grace-Paced Life in a Burnout Culture*. Crossway, 2017.
32. https://www.cnbc.com/2019/03/20/stanford-study-longer-hours-doesnt-make-you-more-productive-heres-how-to-get-more-done-by-doing-less.html AND https://www.brinknews.com/working-fewer-hours-makes-you-more-efficient-heres-the-proof/.
33. Mencken, H. L. *A Mencken Chrestomathy*. New York: Knopf, 1953.
34. See Acts 18:1-3, as well as the comment about Paul at the end of this section.

35. Kuwait, Bahrain, Qatar, Oman, UAE and Saudi Arabia comprise the "Gulf Cooperation Council."
36. I am aware that in some families it is the wife who is fulltime in ministry and tentmaking, while the husband is at home more, along with his own ministry. I am making no value judgments on either model.
37. Redemptive relationships, evangelism: Time spent with the people you're praying to reach for Christ, or time invested seeking to meet people and pursuing relationships. Encounters, relationships, witness. This is outside the workplace. Jason also has relationships at work, and occasional opportunities there to share Christ.

    His Job: Let's imagine that Jason is an associate professor of accounting at the local university. Initially this job was fulltime, but last year he successfully negotiated down his hours.

    Team activities: Team meetings are every other week. There are also some peer-to-peer, one-on-one accountability times, plus one-on-one time with the team leader now and then.

    Further language-learning work: Jason is already relatively fluent but is committed to steady upgrading.

    Other: There is ALWAYS other. Visa things, emails with supporters, planning his week, staring at the wall when the focus is depleted, picking up paperclips, whatever.
38. Aurelius, Marcus. *Meditations*, as republished by Richard Graves, tr. London: Baynes, 1811.

APPENDIX 1: MOVEMENTS AROUND THE WORLD

BY STAN PARKS, DAVE COLES, AND JUSTIN LONG

The 24:14 Vision

In Matthew 24:14, Jesus promised: "This gospel of the kingdom will be proclaimed in the whole world as a testimony to all *ethnē* (people groups), and then the end will come."

In 2017, global leaders from mission organizations, churches, networks and movements committed to reaching the unreached through Church Planting Movements gathered to wrestle with one simple question: "What will it take to pray and work together to start kingdom movements in every unreached people and place in our generation?"

The Holy Spirit directed toward a unified effort to engage the unreached —specifically through CPMs with sacrificial urgency by 2025. This resulted in the launching of a global coalition of like-minded organizations, churches and believers—known as 24:14—to see this God-sized vision fulfilled. As a community, we affirm the unique gifting and calling of every organization and seek to provide information, resources and coordination to facilitate more effective and strategic kingdom movement engagement.

The 24:14 Vision[1] is to see the gospel shared with every people group on earth in our generation. We long to be in the generation that finishes what Jesus began and other faithful workers before us have given their lives to. We know that Jesus waits to return until every people group has an opportunity to respond to the gospel and become part of His Bride.

We recognize the best way to give every people group this opportunity is to see the church started and multiplying in their group. This becomes the best hope for everyone to hear the Good News, as disciples in these multiplying churches are motivated to share the gospel with everyone possible.

These multiplying churches can become what we call a Church Planting Movement (CPM). A CPM is defined as the multiplication of disciples making disciples and leaders developing leaders, resulting in indigenous churches planting churches which begin to spread rapidly through a people group or population segment.

The 24:14 Coalition is not an organization. We are a community of individuals, teams, churches, organizations, networks, and movements who have made a commitment to seeing CPMs in every unreached people and place. Our initial goal is to see effective CPM engagement in every unreached people and place by December 31, 2025.

This means having a team (local, expat or combination) equipped in movement strategy on location in every unreached people and place by that date. We make no claims about when the Great Commission task will be *finished*. That is God's responsibility. He determines the fruitfulness of movements.

We pursue the 24:14 Vision based on four values:

1. Reaching the unreached, in line with Matthew 24:14: bringing the gospel of the Kingdom to every unreached people and place.
2. Accomplishing this **through Church Planting Movements,** involving multiplying disciples, churches, leaders and movements.
3. Acting with a wartime sense of **urgency** to engage every

APPENDIX 1: MOVEMENTS AROUND THE WORLD

unreached people and place with a movement strategy by the end of 2025.

4. Doing these things **in collaboration** with others.

Our vision is to see the gospel of the Kingdom proclaimed throughout the world as a testimony to all people groups **in our lifetime**. We invite you to join us[2] in praying and serving to start kingdom movements in every unreached people and place.

Dimensions of the Harvest

The world's population has risen from 1.6 billion in 1900 to over 7.75 billion today, and will likely exceed 9 billion in the very near future. These billions constitute over 17,400 people groups (cultures and languages), of which 7,400 are unreached and do not have widespread access to the gospel. Some 42% of the world's people make up these people groups—over 3.2 billion unreached, of which 2.2 billion are unevangelized. These billions have the least gospel access of all. Sadly, the number of unevangelized and unreached is currently growing, and will likely reach some 2.7 billion unevangelized by 2050. The church's global efforts to reach the lost have not yet resulted in a widespread trend toward finishing the task of the Great Commission.

The 24:14 Coalition longs to see the good news of salvation blessing these unreached billions. To that end, we work and pray to see every people and place engaged with a CPM effort. We count **engagements** as a team or group of teams focused on starting a movement amongst a specific people group, cluster or language, at any level on the CPM Continuum (1 to 7). Counting this way, we know of **4,500 engagements**.

We count an engagement as a **movement** when it consistently sees four generations of disciples gathered in churches, in multiple streams. Although not every movement has a minimum measure of total disciples, most use the 1,000-believer minimum; even if they don't use that, four generations in multiple streams means a movement would be close to 1,000 believers if not exceeding it. Counting this way, we know of over **1,350 movements**.

Each movement consists of substantial numbers of believers and churches. Getting accurate totals of those is somewhat difficult, because of differences in the ways various movements count believers and/or churches.[3] Based on what we've documented, there are *at least* **77 million believers** in **4.8 million churches** who have come to saving faith in Christ within the past couple of decades (many within just the past few years).

We see the Lord's hand at work in a great many encouraging ways:

We know of over 1,350 church planting movements at CPM levels 5, 6 and 7. [See Graphic #1: The 7-stage CPM Continuum] This is just the number of movements we have been able to verify so far. It's the floor, not the ceiling.

More than half these movements are taking place among Muslims. This is especially encouraging, considering how few Muslims have come to saving faith in Christ during most of the 1400+ years of Islam's history.

The vast majority of these movements are taking place among unreached groups, including some peoples and places that had been considered hardest to reach or most distant from the gospel. We know of approximately 29.5 million former Muslims and 30.49 former Hindus in these movements.

These movements are indigenous—led by people from within the focus culture or a near neighbor culture. These are not led or propped up by distant outsiders, such as directors or finances from the Western world.

These movements are obeying Jesus' command to make disciples of all nations. They are discipling not only their own people, but also reaching out to make disciples among other unreached peoples, often including groups previously unengaged with the gospel.

We know of 2,900 efforts currently at CPM levels 1-4, prayerfully working and moving toward level 5.

The vast majority of these movement efforts are being catalyzed by workers from the Global South. Also, the vast majority of these movements are being started by people from existing movements. One example is the Bhojpuri movement which was begun as a collaboration of outside and inside catalysts. Today, the Bhojpuri movement has been used by God to start movements in eight other language groups in North India without help from outside catalysts.

The 77 million disciples in movements constitute approximately 1% of all people alive today and 2.8% of all followers of Jesus currently alive in the world today. And as movements are, by definition, growing rapidly, this number is also growing rapidly. Movements are the only way we know of that the number of Jesus' disciples grows more rapidly than the population among any given group.

The 4.8 million churches are more than the reported total of all traditional churches globally. The average size of these movement churches is 16, but they are all part of "clusters" of multiple churches united under relationships, common DNA, and connected leadership.

An Illustration:
Movements Starting Movements in the Middle East[4]

When the encrypted message came across my phone I was stunned by its simplicity and boldness, and humbled again by the words of "Harold," my dear friend and partner in the Middle East. Though a former Imam, Al Qaeda terrorist and Taliban leader, his character has been radically transformed by the forgiving power of Jesus. I would trust Harold with my family and my own life—and I have. Together we lead a network of house church movements in 100+ countries called the Antioch Family of Churches.

I had sent Harold a message the day before asking if any of our former Muslim, now Jesus-following brothers and sisters living in Iraq would be willing to help rescue Yazidis. He replied:

"Brother, God has already been speaking to us about this for several months from Hebrews 13:3 (NLT) *'Remember...those being mistreated, as if you felt their pain in your own bodies.'* Are you willing to stand with us in rescuing persecuted Christians and Yazidi minorities from ISIS?"

What could I say? For the last several years our friendship had bonded into a deep commitment to walk the same path with Jesus and work together toward fulfilling the Great Commission. We were working feverishly to train leaders who would multiply our passionate surrender to Jesus, carrying His message of love to the nations. Now Harold was asking me to take another step deeper into rescuing people from slavery to sin and the horrific crimes of ISIS.

I responded: "Yes, Brother, I am ready. Let's see what God will do."

Within hours, teams of trained, experienced local church planters from the Middle East, volunteered to leave their posts to do whatever it would take to rescue these people from ISIS. What we discovered changed our hearts forever.

God was already at work! Broken by the demonic, barbaric actions of ISIS terrorists, Yazidis began pouring into our underground secret locations we called "Community of Hope Refugee Camps." We mobilized teams of local Jesus-followers to provide free medical care, trauma-healing counseling, fresh water, shelter and protection. It was one movement of Jesus-following house churches living out their faith to impact another people.

We also discovered that the best workers came from nearby house churches. They knew the language and culture and had the heartbeat of evangelism and church planting. While other NGOs who registered with the government had to restrict their faith message, our non-formal church-based efforts were filled with prayers, Scripture readings, healings, love and care! And because our team leaders had been lavishly forgiven by Jesus, they lived completely surrendered and filled with courageous boldness.

Soon letters began to pour in:

> *I am from a Yazidi family. For a long time, the condition of my country has been bad because of war. But now it has become worse because of ISIS.*

APPENDIX 1: MOVEMENTS AROUND THE WORLD

Last month they attacked our village. They killed many people and kidnapped me along with other girls. Many of them raped me, treated me like an animal and beat me when I didn't obey their orders. I begged them, "Please don't do this to me," but they smiled and said, "You are our slave." They killed and tortured people many people in front of me.

One day they took me to another place to sell me. My hands were tied, and I was yelling and crying as we walked away from the men who sold me. After 30 minutes, the buyers said, "Dear Sister, God sent us to rescue Yazidi girls from these bad people." Then I saw there were 18 girls they had purchased.

When we arrived in the Community of Hope camp, we understood that God sent His people to save us. We learned that the wives of these men gave up their gold jewelry and paid for us to be free. Now we are safe, learning about God and have a good life.

============

(*From a leader of one of our Community of Hope Refugee Camps.*)

Many Yazidi families have accepted Jesus Christ and have asked to join with our leaders in working and serving their own people. This is very good because they can share with them in their own cultural way. Today, as Jesus-followers we are praying for the affected people that God will provide for their needs and protect them from the Islamic fighters. Please join with us in prayer.

A miracle had begun. A movement of surrendered Jesus-followers from nearby nations—all formerly trapped by Islam—had been freed from their own sin to live for Jesus as their Savior. They were giving their lives to save others. Now, a second movement of Jesus followers has begun among Yazidis.

How could this happen? As D.L. Moody wrote: *"The world has yet to see what God can do with a man fully consecrated to him. By God's help, I aim to be that man."*[5]

Looking to the Future

As we look to the future, we are encouraged by the reality of God at work in our world.

- We are encouraged by the promises of Scripture, which are being fulfilled and have yet to be completed.
- We are encouraged by the astonishing work of salvation coming to so many millions from within unreached groups. We believe God intends to save many more.
- We are encouraged by the miraculous deeds God has been pleased to work by his Spirit, demonstrating his power above all other powers, and his love above all other gods and religious systems. We believe Jesus Christ is the same yesterday, today and forever. We trust he will continue to bless his kingdom's advance with signs and wonders demonstrating that he alone is the true and living God.
- We pray and expect that movements will continue to flourish and multiply disciples, and that hundreds of emerging movements and breakthroughs will continue multiplying to become full-blown movements.
- We pray and expect that by the end of 2025 the Lord of the harvest will have sent movement catalysts into every unreached people and place in the world, planting gospel seeds. We expect that many of those gospel seeds will land of fertile soil, producing a harvest of 30, 60 and 100-fold, for Jesus' glory among all peoples.
- We look forward to seeing the spirit of kingdom collaboration increase among God's people globally.
- We are encouraged that even during the COVID-19 pandemic, many believers in movements have found ways to be a blessing and

a witness to those suffering around them. Many movement leaders have found ways to initiate outreach to additional unengaged groups. The level of commitment, creativity and reliance of God's Spirit that we have seen during these first months of the pandemic encourage us to believe God will continue advancing his kingdom even in the midst of whatever challenges may lie ahead.

- We look forward to the return of the Lord Jesus Christ to fully establish his kingdom on earth. We do not know the time, but we know his promise is trustworthy. So we say, "Maranatha! Come soon, Lord Jesus!"

The 7-stage CPM Continuum

1. **Moving purposefully (G1)** Team on site trying to consistently establish NEW 1st generation believers and churches

2. **Focused (G2)** Some 2nd generation churches (G1 believers started them)

3. **Breakthrough (G3)** Consistent G2 & some G3 churches

4. **Emerging CPM (G4)** Consistent G3 & some G4 churches

 **ESTABLISHED CPM**

5. **CPM** consistent 4th+ generation churches; multiple streams

6. **Sustained CPM** Visionary, indigenous leadership leading the movement with little/no need for outsiders. Stood test of time.

7. **Multiplying CPMs** Catalyzing new CPMs in other unreached peoples and places

---

1. The following is taken from "The 24:14 Vision" by Stan Parks, in *24:14 - A Testimony*, pp. 2-3. Used by permission.
2. For more information, visit 2414now.net.
3. For more information see https://www.justinlong.org/2019/10/15/how-movements-count/.
4. This section is from the article "Surrendered: Movements Start Movements in the Middle East" by "Harold" and William J. Dubois, *Mission Frontiers* January – February 2018, www.missionfrontiers.org, pp. 36-37. Used by permission. "Harold" was born into an Islamic family, raised and schooled to be a radical jihadist and Imam. After his radical conversion to Jesus, Harold used his education, influence and leadership capacity to grow a movement of Jesus Followers. Now, 20+ years later, Harold helps to mentor and lead a network of house church movements among unreached peoples. "William J Dubois" works in highly sensitive areas in which the gospel is spreading powerfully. He and his wife have spent the last 25+ years

training new believers from the harvest to grow in their leadership capacity and multiply house churches among unreached people.
5. Although often erroneously attributed to D. L. Moody himself, he quoted another preacher he heard say these words: Henry Varley. According to Warren Wiersbe in *The Wycliffe Handbook of Preaching and Preachers*, Chicago: Moody Press, 1984, these words were first uttered by Varley in 1873 at an all-night prayer meeting in Dublin at the home of Henry Bewley.

APPENDIX 2: APOSTLESHIP FAQS

As mentioned in the Introduction, we were energized in the 1990s by a number of rediscoveries from New Testament teachings. Here's how I became convinced about **apostleship**:

1. These special words and passages were exactly about what the Lord had called us into a decade earlier, only we didn't realize it back then.

2. That the expansion of the gospel in the New Testament to the nations —following the three widening circles of Acts 1:8[1]—was carried about by apostolic teams.

3. That there were two kinds of apostles, sort of "big A" and "little a." The Twelve were absolutely unique, non-repeatable.[2] But in the early church, a growing number of others were being termed "apostles," both on New Testament pages and elsewhere. Their ministry was to take the gospel to where it had not yet gained a foothold. Also clearly a major part of Jesus' calling for the Twelve was this very same challenge (see below).[3]

4. If there were several apostles of the non-Twelve variety in the New Testament, and if there is no indication that this kind of ministry and calling had ceased, or was somehow limited to the first century, then there must be this same kind of "small a" apostle today. This only makes sense given the swaths of populations on Planet Earth who have yet to hear of

God's grace in Christ and given Jesus' determination that the gospel is preached to all the *ethné*.[4]

5. I even began to observe, just to myself, that several in our organization were likely real-life apostles.

6. It arose from our studies of how New Testament teams were joint efforts of apostles and fellow-workers (Greek *sunergoi*). That seemed also to match our own experience. When in Romans 1:5 Paul says that "we have received grace and apostleship to bring about the obedience of faith for the sake of his name among all the nations," the "we" is likely not just the few unique apostles, but included ALL who were engaged with them in pioneer, apostolic ministry.

7. Instead of relying on the latest missiological buzzwords, it is better if we use the terms our predecessors used in the New Testament (e.g. apostle, fellow workers, the obedience of the peoples, what Christ has accomplished through us, fulfilling the work of the gospel, etc.).

At first, these concepts were controversial, even incendiary. For so long the term **apostle** had been misused and co-opted for other purposes, and no one wanted to touch it. Interestingly, though, when I published *A Vision of the Possible: Pioneer Church Planting in Teams* in 2005-06, various missions and denomination leaders took the initiative to affirm the book specifically because of how it elucidated the whole lost New Testament emphasis on apostleship. Soon some of them wrote excellent whole books on the subject, consistent with the principle of pioneering work to the unreached.[5] When I had first begun writing that book, I felt like I couldn't write a single sentence until I first wrote the appendix concerning the New Testament data on apostles, as a sort of cornerstone to the book.

It would seem that these concepts are no longer controversial today.

FAQ #1 How do we know there continue to be apostles after the first century?

A few decades ago, perhaps most evangelicals were **cessationists**. That is, they were taught and believed that the sign gifts of the Spirit (healings, miracles, prophesy, tongues, etc.) **ceased** soon after the New Testament writing was completed. This made people who didn't like charismatic matters a bit more comfortable. But the problem was that a good biblical argument for this view was non-existent.

It's the same concerning ongoing apostleship throughout the Church Age. I've read the arguments that after the Twelve, Paul, and a few others, there were no more apostles, and personally, I don't believe these arguments hold water. Consider this four-fold case for ongoing and contemporary apostleship:

1. Several New Testament figures are called "apostles" who are not of the Twelve: Barnabas, Paul, Silas, and Timothy. And very possibly also James (brother of Jesus), Andronicus and Junias, and Apollos.[6] Add to this mix the "false apostles" of 2 Corinthians 11:13 and Revelation 2:2. That Paul and John could refer to these is clear evidence that "apostles" were a broader collection of gospel workers—some true and some false—rather than a short, closed list. Paul was unique in his spearheading role to the Gentiles, his visions, and his Scripture-writing. But beyond that, not unique. Indeed, Barnabas is the first non-Twelve apostle named, not Paul. So as H. V. Campenhausen says: "For [Paul] 'the apostles'—and he is deliberately using an existing term—are the foundation-laying preachers of the Gospel, missionaries and church founders possessing the full authority of Christ and belong to a bigger circle in no way confined to the Twelve."[7]
2. Jesus told the eleven apostles in Acts 1:8, *"But you will receive power when the Holy Spirit has come upon you, and you will be my witnesses in **Jerusalem** and in all **Judea and Samaria**, and to **the end of the earth**."* As the reader may be aware, this threefold expansion of the gospel is pretty much the outline for the Book of Acts of the Apostles. We know how this was fulfilled in the book by non-Twelve apostles as much or more than by the Twelve.
3. It would not make sense for Paul—writing in the early AD 60s—

to include apostles in the five-fold leadership ministry of Ephesians 4:11 if he was only thinking of the 12 Apostles.
4. There is not a single New Testament verse that even hints at such a cessation of this crucial function (unless one argues that the requirements of Acts 1:21-22 apply to all small 'a' apostles—an argument that does not hold up. See *Do All Apostles Have to Have Seen Jesus?* below).

And why would we think for a moment that apostleship has ceased, when so much of the world will be desperately unreached up until Christ's return?

FAQ #2 Is apostleship a gift or a calling?

As we saw in Romans 1:1, clearly it is a calling. This has led some to assert that it is therefore not a gifting as well. While there is no explicit "gift of apostleship" mentioned in the New Testament, I believe it does come with special **gifting**. Consider:

1. Apostles are **given** to the church (Ephesians 4:11).
2. Believers are given abilities by the Spirit to effectively carry out whatever work they are supposed to do (1 Corinthians 12:4-6). Likewise in 1 Corinthians 12:28 apostles are listed, and this in the overall context of God calling and equipping His people for His works.
3. As we saw earlier, Paul "received grace" (Romans 1:5. Gk. *charis*) to effectively carry out his ministry. This word is similar to the nomenclature of gifts (Gk. *charismata*) in 1 Corinthians 12.
4. Looking over the New Testament—especially looking at what apostles were to accomplish, and from my observations—I believe the prominent necessary spiritual abilities of apostles are pioneering, teaching and leadership. "Pioneering" would include that unstoppable-ness, undeterrable focus, grit, spiritual entrepreneurship, and the righteous ambition Paul speaks of in Romans 15, not to mention that must-go to "where Christ is not named" inner beacon.

Undoubtedly the "gift mixes" and personalities of apostles will vary widely. For example, Paul was driven and task-oriented; Barnabas—whose name means "son of encouragement"—was strongly pastoral and probably had robust encouragement and mercy gifts; Timothy was shy, but phenomenally steady and faithful. Apollos was winsome.[8]

FAQ #3 Aren't Apostles supposed to lay foundations?

Yes. Absolutely. Especially the Twelve, as Paul says in Ephesians 2:19-20, *"So then you are no longer strangers and aliens, but you are fellow citizens with the saints and members of the household of God, built on the foundation of the apostles and prophets, Christ Jesus himself being the cornerstone."*

But this is not contrary to pioneering. A leader in the NewFrontiers Together movement explains it well:

> Paul gives a strong emphasis to this in 1 Corinthians - what he had done as a wise master builder - and in practice, all his corrective teaching effectively appeals to the foundation that he had laid amongst them. The church is built upon the foundation of the apostles and prophets and though that relates to the revelation of truth expressed in the New Testament, those foundations still need laying in each church as it is planted. Church foundation laying is a very important part of church planting and the apostolic ministry is vital in that context. However, it is not laying a foundation just in a pastoral or teaching sense but rather apostolic ministry ensures a foundation is laid that can rapidly reproduce itself. It is therefore appropriate to the culture in which it is laid as well as containing the New Testament revelation of the fulfillment of God's plans in Christ for the whole world. Apostolic foundation laying is reproducible so Paul repeats on several occasions the fact that when he planted churches, those churches were multiplied through indigenous leadership into that region, e.g. in Thessalonica (1 Thessalonians 1), in Corinth where the gospel spread throughout Achaia, e.g. into places like Cenchreae.[9]

And, as noted above, we see the same dynamic in the Ephesus ministry.

FAQ #4 What about "Timothy-type" apostles? And can you train someone to be an apostle?

In 1 Thessalonians 2:5-7 Paul reviews with his Thessalonian readers how it was that they became a church: *"For we never came with flattering speech, as you know, nor with a pretext for greed—God is witness—nor did we seek glory from men, either from you or from others, even though as apostles of Christ we might have asserted our authority. But we proved to be gentle among you..."* There can be little doubt that the "we" refers to the listed authors of the letter—Paul, Silas, and Timothy—who were, indeed, the co-founders of the church.

Timothy, an **apostle**? Isn't this the guy who tended to put his morning workouts ahead of his quiet times? Who twice had to be admonished not to forget or neglect the special spiritual gift everyone agreed he had? Who was the only person in the New Testament **encouraged** to increase his alcohol intake? Was this because of his continual inclination toward fear and timidity? Paul was not ashamed of the gospel and revealed that suffering was a natural part of the job, but Timothy had to be exhorted not to be ashamed or shrink back from suffering. We see how Paul had to pave the way for his arrival at Corinth by instructing them to *"see that he is with you without cause to be afraid, for he is doing the Lord's work, as I also am. So let no one despise him."* (1 Corinthians 16:10-11) Would we normally think an apostle needs such kid-glove treatment?

The point is, if there are Timothy apostles, then that should give much encouragement to many of us who feel less than Paul-like in terms of fearlessness, laser-beam focus, and nothing-can-stop-me ambition for our particular people group!

It also means we may need more apostolic mentoring on the field. While I do not believe that apostleship gifting can be created out of nothing. So Timothy must have had at least a latent calling and gifting as an apostle that matured over years through Paul's mentoring.

FAQ #5 Are all field workers "apostles"?

If "apostle" means "sent one," then all who are sent by a church and who get on a plane are apostles, right? Wrong. We cannot simply go by the etymology of a word but must look at its meaning in context. Very clearly in the New Testament apostle was a special title and only referred to a few who had a certain special calling and ministry. Of the approximately 30 people mentioned by name in the New Testament as going out for the spread of the gospel—usually long-term, itinerant, and financially supported, only maybe a fifth of these are called apostles, though we can't be sure. Anyway, it was a special title, used sparingly, and it was often unclear who was or was not an apostle.

FAQ #6 Is it biblical to use the adjective "apostolic"?

The word apostle is not used as an adjective in the New Testament. And yet in English, in the 21st century, it is much easier to use the adjective than the noun. George Miley astutely observes:

> The word *apostle* might trigger more concern in some than the word *apostolic* or even the compound *apostolic-type*. Notice the difference between saying, "He is an apostle," "He is an apostolic leader," or, "He is an apostolic-type leader." Similarly, we can speak of apostolic ministry or even apostolic-type ministry. If we have hesitations about the role of the apostle today, using the adjective might give us more freedom to talk openly about this subject.[10]

So, is this a legitimate use of language, or mere cowardice on our part? I believe that it is legitimate. Of the four occurrences of the Greek for *apostleship*, ESV has it as an adjective in one of them (Galatians 2:8), and of the other three the adjective could be used.

FAQ #7 Do all apostles have to have seen Jesus?

Some believe this must be a requirement from Acts 1:21-22. But that is only regarding replacing Judas. That person (Matthias) would become one of the Twelve. The context shows that staying with merely 11 would be inadequate, and that having 13 would be too many (as otherwise, they could have appointed Matthias AND Justus). It was only for Judas' big 'A' replacement, not the small 'a' others in the New Testament.

FAQ #8 Do apostles have to write scripture?

This question begs the response: "404 error not found."

I'm not sure where that comes from. John 14:26 perhaps. But most of those identified as apostles did not write Scripture. And not all of the New Testament was written by apostles. Believing in modern-day pioneer apostles does not imply that they have authority to write Scripture. That's a non-sequitur.

FAQ #9 Are *signs and wonders* a necessary mark?

As Paul explains to his Roman readers, the remarkable and expansive results of his apostolic ministry were **powered** by two things: signs and wonders, and the Holy Spirit (Romans 15:19). This was *"what Christ has accomplished through me"* as an apostle. In 1 Corinthians 9:2, Paul has to plead with the Corinthian church not to reject him but to recognize and respect that he is not just *an* apostle, but *their* apostle. He implores them to think back to how they came into existence as a church of Jesus Christ, and how God validated his apostleship in their midst, *"The signs of a true apostle were performed among you with all perseverance, by signs and wonders and miracles."*

Likewise, throughout the centuries Christ's pioneer gospel ambassadors have frequently performed amazing miracles as God was authenticating their authority among people hostile to the message, through healings, authority over demons, even nature miracles, and raising people from the dead. Be encouraged! Whether you're Pentecostal or Presbyterian, God will likely give some amazing answers to prayer as you pray for people in Jesus' name. We saw some miraculous healings in Jordan—which were affirmed by our local friends—even though a healing ministry was not in our background. Apostolic teams should pray for this and expect it.

The question arises, is this an **essential** sign of apostleship? Or, to put it another way, if someone appears to be an apostle in every other way but has never performed a miracle, does that mean they are not an apostle? I don't think we can settle this question completely among us, and there is certainly room for different opinions. Personally speaking, while I think that many of our effective apostolic teams will witness some of the miraculous, I do not believe it will always be an essential sign. It is a common sign, but not an indispensable one. Miracles are not mentioned in every New Testament apostolic ministry. And they are present in some other ministries that are not necessarily by an apostle (e.g. Stephen, Philip).

FAQ #10 Doesn't the Greek of Matthew 28:19 actually say that we are supposed to "disciple all the nations" instead of "make disciples of all the nations"?

Some might say, "Most translations have it 'make disciples of all nations.' But the 'of' is not in the Greek text; 'all nations' is in the accusative, and so that means that 'all nations' is the direct object of 'make disciples' We are therefore supposed to mainly pursue the transformation of the entire nation or ethnolinguistic group." Perhaps some of your high school grammar is coming back to you from the fog.

There is good reason why all major modern translations have it as **make disciples of all nations**, i.e. go for disciple-making in every nation, leading individuals, families, and social groups to follow Jesus (and thus form into growing and reproducing faith communities). Including 'of' is necessary to make accurate sense of the verb into English. Realistically 100% of a nation isn't going to believe and follow, and besides, you couldn't fit an entire country into a baptismal pool.

Here's the reason why it is so important to not misinterpret this: Those who see it this way, tend to view transforming even the secular society of a nation as important or more important than evangelism and church planting. As a result humanitarian projects take on an out-of-proportion role. It's as if the missionaries can go in and help a corrupt society become a little less corrupt, then they've fulfilled 28:19. Societal change, rather than leading people to become true Christ-followers in faith communities, becomes the goal.

So should apostolic workers seek to improve people's lives, work out Christ's love in practical ways with His compassion, confront social injustice, or promote reconciliation, even between unbelieving groups? Yes. As John Piper puts it, "We care about all suffering now, especially eternal suffering later." And many may feel called specifically to humanitarian ministry **rather than** apostolic work, and that is great for those so called. Even in apostolic ministries, these efforts can oftentimes play a strong role in demonstrating the gospel, while the primary focus is on birthing reproducing churches, and the spread of the Good News. We must keep in view how the Twelve and all the small "a" apostles interpreted the Apostolic Directive and what they did in obedience. Some will point out that time and again when the church begins to take form among a people group and multiplies, the transformation of the lives of Christ-followers results in a general uplift in society, even as the believers prove to be salt and light. One thinks, for example, of the staggering transformation of Ireland as a result of Patrick's ministry. It was a wonderful by-product in the society of the leavening of the gospel, but it was not the objective. It doesn't even always happen. In fact, initially, gospel breakthroughs might produce more societal distress, as persecution breaks out against believers and families are pulled apart. Let us not forget the terrible persecution of the new churches in either Somalia or Afghanistan in the 20th century, and how those countries spiraled downward and have yet to recover.[11]

It's a question of biblical priority and an accurate understanding of the Apostolic Directive.

FAQ #11 Are there female apostles?

This is easy to answer. "I don't know." Indeed, it would be impossible to make a strong case either way simply from New Testament data. The only apostles mentioned are men, unless you take Romans 16:7 to refer to a woman apostle: *"Greet Andronicus and Junias, my kinsmen and my fellow prisoners, who are outstanding among the apostles..."* The problem here is Junias might be a man's name, as some scholars believe. And it is not clear how to translate the phrase *"outstanding among the apostles"* (Gk. *en tois apostolois*). For example, the ESV has it as "well known to the apostles." There is plenty of room on this question for different viewpoints among apostolic workers.

What is beyond debate is how women gospel workers have played extraordinarily pivotal roles in the spread of the gospel throughout history and today.

1. Acts 1:8 But you will receive power when the Holy Spirit has come upon you, and you will be my witnesses *in Jerusalem and in all Judea and Samaria, and to the end of the earth.*
2. Whose name will be written on the twelfth foundation stone of the New Jerusalem? (Revelation 21:14) Matthias?
3. As William McBirnie makes clear in his very helpful *The Search for the Twelve Apostles*, sooner or later they all went out across the world with Jesus' message. Even in 1st century Judea and Samaria they were doing ground-breaking work, as those areas were certainly not reached.
4. Greek for "nations."
5. Dent, Don. *The Ongoing Role of Apostles in Missions: The Forgotten Foundation.* Bloomington, IN: Westbow Press, 2019. AND Devenish, David. *Fathering Leaders, Motivating Mission: Restoring the Role of the Apostle in Today's Church.* Authentic Media, 2011.
6. Epaphroditus and the financial trustees of 2 Corinthians 8:23 clearly had secondary roles. They were *sent* from the churches, rather than being termed *apostles of Christ*. In these cases *apostolos* is best translated as *messenger* or *representative*.
7. Brown, Colin ed. *Dictionary of New Testament Theology Vol.1.* "Apostle." Grand Rapids, MI: Zondervan Publishing House, 1980.
8. See 1 Corinthians 3:4ff; 4:6 and 4:9 regarding Apollos' likely apostleship.
9. Devenish, *Fathering Leaders*.
10. George Miley, *Loving the Church...Blessing the Nations*. Waynesboro, GA: Authentic, 2003, 96.
11. In various YouTube videos Nik Ripken shares about their many years in Somalia, and the devastation brought on the nascent church of Somalia (of Muslim-background believers). Slowly, through a steady progression of martyrdoms, the number of believers he was aware of went from 150 down to four. Incredibly heart-breaking.

APPENDIX 3: JESUS' SENDING OUT THE 12 AND THE 72

Sending of the 12 and the 72

Matthew 10:5-15 (11) The Twelve	Mark 6:7-13 (7) The Twelve	Luke 9:1-6 (6) The Twelve	Luke 10:1-12 (12) The Seventy-two
	⁷ And he called the twelve and began to send them out two by two,	¹ And he called the twelve together	¹ After this the Lord appointed seventy-two others and sent them on ahead of him, two by two, into every town and place where he himself was about to go.
A ⁵ These twelve Jesus sent out, instructing them, "Go nowhere among the Gentiles and enter no town of the Samaritans, ⁶ but go rather to the lost sheep of the house of Israel.			**A** ² And he said to them, "The harvest is plentiful, but the laborers are few. Therefore pray earnestly to the Lord of the harvest to send out laborers into his harvest. ³ Go your way; behold, I am sending you out as lambs in the midst of wolves.
⁷ And proclaim as you go, saying, 'The kingdom of heaven is at hand.' **B** ⁸ Heal the sick, raise the dead, cleanse lepers, cast out demons.	and gave them authority over the unclean spirits.	and gave them power and authority over all demons and to cure diseases, ² and he sent them out to proclaim the kingdom of God and to heal.	
C You received without paying; give without pay. ⁹ Acquire no gold nor silver nor copper for your belts, ¹⁰ no bag for your journey, nor two tunics nor sandals nor a staff, for the laborer deserves his food.	⁸ He charged them to take nothing for their journey except a staff: no bread, no bag, no money in their belts- ⁹ but to wear sandals and not put on two tunics.	³ And he said to them, "Take nothing for your journey, no staff, nor bag, nor bread nor money; and do not have two tunics.	**C** ⁴ Carry no moneybag, no knapsack, no sandals, and greet no one on the road.
			⁵ Whatever house you enter, first say, 'Peace be to this house!' ⁶ And if a son of peace is there, your peace will rest upon him. But if not, it will return to you.
D ¹¹ And whatever town or village you enter, find out who is worthy in it and stay there until you depart. ¹² As you enter the house, greet it. ¹³ And if the house is worthy, let your peace come upon it, but if it is not worthy, let your peace return to you.	¹⁰ And he said to them, "Whenever you enter a house, stay there until you depart from there.	⁴ And whatever house you enter, stay there, and from there depart.	**D** ⁷ And remain in the same house, eating and drinking what they provide, for the laborer deserves his wages. Do not go from house to house. ⁸ Whenever you enter a town and they receive you, eat what is set before you.
			B ⁹ Heal the sick in it and say to them, 'The kingdom of God has come near to you.'
E ¹⁴ And if anyone will not receive you or listen to your words, shake off the dust from your feet when you leave that house or town. ¹⁵ Truly, I say to you, it will be more bearable on the day of judgment for the land of Sodom and Gomorrah than for that town.	¹¹ And if any place will not receive you and they will not listen to you, when you leave, shake off the dust that is on your feet as a testimony against them."	⁵ And wherever they do not receive you, when you leave that town shake off the dust from your feet as a testimony against them."	¹⁰ But whenever you enter a town and they do not receive you, go into its streets and say, ¹¹ 'Even the dust of your town that clings to our feet we wipe off against you. Nevertheless know this, that the kingdom of God has come near.' **E** ¹² I tell you, it will be more bearable on that day for Sodom than for that town.
F	¹² So they went out and proclaimed that people should repent. ¹³ And they cast out many demons and anointed with oil many who were sick and healed them.	⁶ And they departed and went through the villages, preaching the gospel and healing everywhere.	

APPENDIX 4: EXAMPLES OF SHEMA STATEMENTS

1. My company's purpose is to glorify God.
2. We also fast and pray.
3. We came to ____ because God wanted us to.
4. Can we pray for you?
5. Her name is a biblical name and has biblical meaning.
6. Beards and tattoos draw people in.
7. We pray for people and needs.
8. Which is more important: *salāt* or *duʿāʾ*?
9. The Lord may give healing, words of knowledge, or prophetic words.
10. Have you ever had a dream you thought was from God?
11. I'd love to hear the Arab (or whatever) perspective on this book or idea.
12. What would your family or friends think of this?
13. What will happen to you when you die?
14. Ladies: Covering your head can lead to good discussions.

15. God loves you. God is love.

16. What does it mean, *Bismillah*...? (or other question)

17. Who is God to you? What are you learning from God this week?

18. Share proverbs and parables—tell stories.

19. Which man who was praying in the Temple went away justified?

20. Children are a blessing from God. I can raise them up to serve God.

21. Our marriage is different because we follow Jesus.

22. I read in the Bible recently...

23. Share the Christian *salat* (The Lord's Prayer) with them.

24. Please explain to me this expression in your culture...

25. *Ahl al-kitāb*—a person of the book—the Quran says to listen to these people.

26. I'd be interested to hear what your family or friends think about this?

27. Why did I come here? I'll tell you...

28. Share what you prayed about today. Or learned in your QT.

29. Share how God has worked in your life recently.

APPENDIX 5: A TYPICAL DBS MEETING

START-UP

Q1: What are you thankful for this week?

Q2: What trouble are you having this week?

Facilitator or other **prays** (short, simple & focused).

Review the previous DBS. This might be more important than the new passage. One or two briefly retell(s) the previous story/passage. Each retells what their 'Obey' step was (Q5), and how it went this last week.

NEW BIBLE STUDY

Read the new passage. Each person shares what they think it means. One or two can "retell" it, and the group discusses questions for understanding (with Facilitator keeping things simple and on-track).

Q3: What does this passage teach me about God? (things such as about his character, what he loves, what he hates, how he works, etc.) Go around the group, and each person shares only one thing at a time.

Q4: What does this passage teach me about man? (e.g. weaknesses, strengths, needs, ways to grow, thinking to change, etc.)

Q5: Since (or 'if') this is the word of God...How will I obey and apply this to my life? Obedience is the evidence of Faith and the means of successful living. Q5 and Q7 are the two most important questions.

CLOSING

Q6: How can we help each other this week?

Q7: Who will I tell what I am learning about God this week? Probably the most important question. ["No Q7 = No DMM"]

Conclude by letting each person **share** a stress or need or problem he/she or a friend has. Then take turns **praying** for each other. Or pair up.

APPENDIX 6: SAMPLE OF DBS LESSON SETS

These are borrowed from a DMM ministry in Iraq and are adapted there into three different languages. Each lesson has an associated Bible passage.

SET 1 - DISCOVERY

Story 1: Creation and Fall of Man

Story 2: Abraham's Faith

Story 3a: Moses and the Passover

Story 3b: Moses and the Law of Sacrifice

Story 4: Prophecy of the Savior's Coming

Story 5: The Birth of Jesus Christ

Story 6: Jesus' Healing Power

Story 7: The Death and Resurrection of Jesus the Messiah

Story 8: New Birth and Salvation

SET 2 - DECISION

Lesson 1: Faith, Confession and the Cost of Following Jesus

Lesson 2: Repentance, Baptism, and the Gift of the Holy Spirit

SET 3 - DISCIPLESHIP

Lesson 1: Vine and Shepherd

Lesson 2: Who are We?

Lesson 3: Abiding

Lesson 4: "Showing Yourselves to be My disciples"

Lesson 5: "Love the Lord your God"

Lesson 6: "Love your Neighbor as Yourself"

Lesson 7: "A Servant is not Greater than his Master"

Lesson 8: "Go and Bear fruit"

SET 4 - CHURCH DECISION SET

Lesson 1: Unity and the Body of Christ

Lesson 2: Breaking of Bread

SET 5 - CHURCH

Lesson 1: The Source of our Learning

Lesson 2: Worshiping God

Lesson 3: Prayer

Lesson 4: Generosity

Lesson 5: Sharing Jesus with Others

Lesson 6: Gathering Together

APPENDIX 7: THE STORY OF ALMA

When people are coming to faith in Christ in societies with very different religious traditions, there usually is no more urgent question in their minds than that of **identity**. Here we find Alma's account so very relevant. As told by Anna Travis.

> I have had the privilege of knowing a Muslim woman I will call Alma for the last 15 years. Alma flows in God's grace as she introduces Isa al-Masih (Jesus the Messiah) to family members and fellow Muslims. In the years I have known her, Alma has seen several hundred come to know Jesus as Savior and risen Lord, just as she has. In addition, working with a handful of other Muslim followers of Jesus, she has planted a network of more than 20 Jesus-centered home fellowships (i.e. house churches). One important part of Alma's spiritual journey and this network of Muslim believers is that none of them has "changed religions" as they have embraced the Good News. Although they hold to several beliefs that make them different from typical Muslims (such as believing in the death and resurrection of Jesus), they have remained Muslims culturally, socially, and legally.
>
> Alma herself had become a follower of Isa five years before my husband and I met her. Before choosing to follow Jesus, she had studied the Bible for many months, at times with her Christian employer. At the same

time she was studying Scripture, her teenage son became very ill and was hospitalized. A Christian went to the hospital and prayed for her son in Jesus' name. God miraculously healed him. Between the healing and what she was reading in the Bible, Alma was inwardly wanting to follow Jesus.

In the Asian city where Alma lives, there are numerous churches and thousands of Christians from other areas who have migrated to her city. As Christians whom Alma knew found out that she was reading the Bible and interested in Jesus, quite a few of them invited her to join their church and be baptized. For years she politely refused. She loved Jesus and appreciated her friendship with them, but never felt God directing her to "change religions" and/or join one of the many churches in her city.

Not long after her son's healing, she met an Asian believer visiting her country who had heard of Alma's interest in Jesus. One day he respectfully asked her what she thought about Jesus and the Bible. It was clear from her answers that Alma felt drawn to Jesus and believed everything the Bible said, even including the account of his sacrificial death and resurrection. (Nearly all Muslims reject this.) Sensitively the Asian visitor then asked her if she had become a follower of Jesus. She replied, "No." He was surprised by the answer; it seemed to him she wanted to follow Jesus, but he could tell something was holding her back. The longer they talked, the more the reason became apparent. Alma loved Jesus and the Bible but had been led to believe that following Jesus was "off limits" for a Muslim.

Realizing the dilemma, the visitor said, "Please listen Alma—I am a pastor. I think I understand what you are saying. You need to know this important truth—Jesus is for everyone, not only for Christians. If you believe Jesus died and rose again and you confess your sins and your need for what God has done through Jesus, you can become his follower right now. Please understand that we are saved by Jesus and not by religion."

They spoke a while longer and then prayed, as Alma declared her decision to follow Isa. She describes this experience as the day the Spirit of God entered her heart. She went home and shared with her teenage son (who had also been reading the Bible). "Son, we are saved by Jesus, not religion—you can declare your faith in him and begin following him right now." Soon after, her son decided to follow Jesus, and then her mother did as well.

Alma then started reading the Bible regularly with several other Muslim women who had been on a similar spiritual journey. When Alma and I met about five years later, we became friends and started meeting regularly to pray and talk about life. We prayed together for healing from emotional wounds she had received in her youth, as well as for freedom from spiritual oppression.

Over the next few months, Alma sensed God whispering in her heart, encouraging her to bring the message of Jesus to others in the community as she had done with her son and mother.

The Lord led her in a unique way of doing this. Because Muslims technically believe in four Holy Books (the *Taurat, Zabur, Injil,* and *Qur'an*),[1] she would ask them which of the four they had read. Most would say, "One—the Qur'an—isn't that all that is needed?" In her winsome way, however, if she thought there was any interest, she would continue, "OK, but haven't you ever wondered what's in the *Taurat, Zabur,* and *Injil?*" (These three names are Arabic terms for the Jewish and Christians Scriptures – the books Muslims believe God sent before the Qur'an.[2]) Most would say, "No, I am not interested, and you shouldn't be either!" But some did show an interest. It seemed that through her light-hearted approach, mixed with the fact that she had known most of these neighbors for decades, she was able to ask questions like this, one Muslim to another, without offending. The net result was that within a short period there was a group of about ten Muslim friends studying the *Injil* (the New Testament) with her.

Over the next few months, this initial group of ten grew to twenty people. Shortly thereafter a second group was formed. Over the next two years, these initial two groups grew to eight and eventually more than twenty home fellowships.

The groups meet in homes. They typically read one chapter of the Bible per week and discuss how God is leading them to apply it to their lives. They pray for each other, chat for a while, and close with a simple snack. Nearly all of those who participate in a home gathering for more than a few months end up deciding to receive Jesus as Savior and to follow him with all their heart. Alma and other senior leaders of this network appoint their leaders for the home fellowships. To my knowledge, none has ever changed religions nor attended existing churches in the city, although Alma and others have had significant spiritual input from understanding Christians. I am deeply moved by the godliness of the members of these fellowships whom I have known either before or after their journey with Jesus began.

As they study God's Word, there are some Muslim beliefs they reject and others they transform, modify or marginalize. In their daily lifestyle (diet, clothing, language, personal names, community associations, and holidays), their lives are like other Muslims in their community. The differences that now exist are seen in the areas of inward changes of the heart—such as more peace and joy—and Biblical faithfulness in their treatment of others—such as forgiving others, and helping and showing kindness to neighbors they formerly disliked. Much like a citizen with two passports, they see themselves culturally, socially, and legally as Muslims in their community and context, and also citizens of heaven and part of the body of Christ through their relationship with Isa the Messiah.

---

1. These are, respectively, the Torah, the Psalms, the Gospel or New Testament and the Qur'an.
2. Though the Bible is technically viewed as Scripture by Muslims, tragically, a belief became widespread around the year 1050 AD and now is believed by nearly all Muslims, that somehow the Bible was altered after it was declared to be Holy Scripture. This heart-breaking misunderstanding has prevented nearly all Muslims from reading the Bible at all.

APPENDIX 8: HANDLING LOTS OF EMAIL

Remember Nicole? Let's imagine that she receives around 40 emails per day on average. Some of these are truly important, and from people in her life she wants to honor with timely responses. Others of these are unimportant or trivial: promotions from businesses she's not yet ready to unsubscribe from, postings on a discussion board she doesn't need to review very often if ever, some business asking for survey feedback, etc. Other messages are things you want to read (e.g. someone's prayer letter), but just not right now. Still others she should politely respond to even if it is simply, "Sorry, I don't think I can help you with that right now."

Here's what we're trying to accomplish: **We want Nicole to cut her email time in half and yet lose nothing important.** This is the same method as explained in the chapter, but with a bit more detail. **By going through her Inbox once a day, fully and relatively quickly, and therefore having an EMPTY Inbox (Imagine!), she remains mentally free and uncluttered and can keep giving creative focus to the things that are of highest priority in her life.** Here is the super-simple method. Just three steps (if you don't count the "Do Not's" (1 and 4).

1. DO NOT create topical folders, or folders by person, to put your emails into when you've finished with them. This is one of the biggest time-wasting traps that so many people fall into. But you say, "I may need to find a certain email a year from now. I won't be able to do so without topical/person folders." Not true. I use the email client (app) Mozilla Thunderbird. It has a powerful Search function, which I have saved and named "Find INCOMING"; and I use it all the time. I've never been unable to find a message I wanted quickly, even going back years. I can search by From (or CC), or Subject, or Age, or Size, or text in the body of the message, or other parameters. Ninety percent of the time I'm searching by From, and then just sort by age. That's Thunderbird, but virtually every email app has something similar. Of course, sometimes what you need to find is your Outgoing message to someone, which is likewise easy to search for.

2. DO create monthly folders for all your Incoming. E.g. 20 09 (for September 2020), 22 01 (for January 2022), etc. I've got these going back over 7 years![1] I don't know how much space this takes up, and I don't care (see #4 below).[2]

3. DO: Once a day—and this requires self-control to keep it to that—completely but quickly go through your Inbox.[3] What does "Go through" actually mean? This is the crux of the method. Sort your Inbox from oldest to newest. I have the newest at the top, but whatever floats your boat. Then I start at the bottom (oldest). After dealing with each email, which is normally very fast, I hit the 'B' key and it takes me to the next message in the queue without returning to the main screen. Again, that's Thunderbird, but every app has a key or button or something to go to the next message.

How do you deal with each email? Again, this is crucial. **You follow the 3-minute rule.**[4] So many messages do not warrant any response. Many you can see what it is in 5 seconds and move on (for me, hitting the 'B' key). Others need a response. **If you can deal with it in 3 minutes or less, go ahead**. If it is going to take more time than that, create a task for it in your Tasks System. That way it will not fall through the cracks, you won't need to expend any mental energy remembering that you need to get back with Joe, and you will deal with it at some point, whether sooner or later, with the appropriate level of priority. Simple!

If I come home from a trip and have 253 emails in my Inbox, I don't groan, and I don't throw them all away and hope for the best. Rather, I can generally process about 100 per hour. So after a trip with a bloated Inbox, in around 2½ hours I am back on top of my emails, and they are not on top of me.

4. DO NOT spend any time deciding what messages to keep and which ones to discard.[5] Doing so is not worth your time. And hard disc space, whether on your laptop or in the cloud, is plentiful and cheap. Don't give it another thought.

5. DO: At the end of this process, move all your Inbox messages—which you have reviewed all of them—to this month's folder.

But let us say that you would like to try this—to be happy and carefree in your **email-life** like Nicole, having an empty Inbox each day—but you are starting out with 18,546 emails in your Inbox going back a few years. What to do? Should you create monthly folders going back years and move them all into those? I would not bother. Rather, I'd create monthly folders for the current year, and yearly folders for everything before the current year. Then move all the Inbox emails into the appropriate folders. This shouldn't take much time.

---

1. Also, if your Sent box is becoming too large, you can eventually move them into two sent folders per year, e.g. "Sent 2018A," "Sent 2018B" and so forth.
2. See Chapter 7, "Organizing: Setting up the right buckets, in Allen, *Getting Things Done*.
3. See Chapter 6, "Processing: Getting "In" to Empty," in Allen, *Getting Things Done*.
4. Or you can make a 2-minute or 4-minute rule; but right in that range only.
5. Unless perhaps there's a 20 MB pointless advert.

BIBLIOGRAPHY

Allen, David. *Getting Things Done: The Art of Stress-Free Productivity.* New York, NY: Penguin Books, 2001.

Allen, Roland. *Missionary Methods: St. Paul's or Ours?* Grand Rapids, MI: Wm. B. Eerdmans, 1962.

Allen, Roland. *Spontaneous Expansion of the Church.* Grand Rapids, MI: Wm. B. Eerdmans, 1962.

Blanchard, Kenneth. Johnson, Spenser. *The One Minute Manager.* Berkley Books, 1981.

Cahill, Thomas. *How the Irish Saved Civilization: The Untold Story of Ireland's Heroic Role From the Fall of Rome to the Rise of Medieval Europe.* Anchor. 1996.

Chesterton, G. K. *Orthodoxy.* Peabody, MA: Hendrickson, 2006.

Cho, Paul Yong-Gi. *Successful Home Cell Groups.* Logos Associates, 1987.

Cloud, Henry and Townsend, John. *Boundaries: When to Say Yes, How to Say No To Take Control of Your Life.* Updated ed. Zondervan, 2017.

Cordeiro, Wayne. *Leading on Empty: Refilling Your Tank and Renewing Your Passion*. Bethany House, 2010.

Dent, Don. *The Ongoing Role of Apostles in Missions: The Forgotten Foundation*. Bloomington, IN: Westbow Press, 2019.

Devenish, David. *Fathering Leaders, Motivating Mission: Restoring the Role of the Apostle in Today's Church*. Authentic Media, 2011.

Garrison, David. *A Wind in the House of Islam: How God is Drawing Muslims Around the World to Faith in Jesus Christ*. Monument, CO: WIGTake Resources, 2014.

Garrison, David. *Church Planting Movements: How God Is Redeeming A Lost World*. Monument, CO: WIGTake Resources, 2004.

Griessman, E. Eugene. *Time Tactics of Very Successful People*. McGraw-Hill Education, 1994.

Hay, Alex Rattray. *The Functioning Church and Church-Planter of the New Testament*. Audubon, NJ: New Testament Missionary Union, 1947.

Hay, Alex Rattray. *The New Testament Order for Church and Missionary*. Audubon, NJ: New Testament Missionary Union, 1978.

Hettinga, Jan David. *Follow Me: Experience the Loving Leadership of Jesus*. NavPress, 1996.

John, Victor. *Bhojpuri Breakthrough: A Movement that Keeps Multiplying*. WIGTake Resources. 2019.

Johnson, Lynn D. *Enjoy Life! Healing with Happiness*. Head Acre Press, 2007.

Latourette, Kenneth Scott. *A History of the Expansion of Christianity*. 7 vols. New York: Harper and Row, 1937-45.

Leatherwood, Rick. "Mongolia: As a People Movement to Christ Emerges, What Lessons Can We Learn?" in *Mission Frontiers* July-August 1998.

Lin, David and Spaulding, Steve, eds. *Sharing Jesus in the Buddhist World*. Pasadena, CA: William Carey Library, 2003.

Livingstone, Greg. *Planting Churches in Muslim Cities. A Team Approach*. Grand Rapids, MI: Baker Books, 1993.

Lucado, Max. *Anxious for Nothing: Finding Calm in a Chaotic World*. Thomas Nelson, 2019.

Mandryk, Jason. *Operation World: The Definitive Prayer Guide to Every Nation*. IVP Books, 2010.

Marantika, Chris. *Principles & Practice of World Mission—Including a Closer Look in an Islamic Context*. Indonesia: Iman Press, 2002.

McBirnie, William Steuart. *The Search for the Twelve Apostles*. Carol Stream, IL: Tyndale Momentum, 1973.

McGavran, Donald A. *Ethnic Realities and the Church: Lessons from India*. Pasadena, CA: William Carey Library, 1979.

McGavran, Donald A. *Understanding Church Growth*. Grand Rapids, MI: Eerdmans, 1980.

Miley, George. *Loving the Church...Blessing the Nations*. Waynesboro, GA: Gabriel Publishing, 2003.

Murray, David. *Reset: Living a Grace-Paced Life in a Burnout Culture*. Crossway, 2017.

Neighbor, Ralph W. *Where Do We Go from Here?: A Guidebook for the Cell Group Church*. Rev. ed. Touch Outreach Ministries, 2000.

Neill, Stephen. *A History of Christian Missions*. New York: Penguin, 1964.

Newport, Cal. *Deep Work: Rules for Focused Success in a Distracted World*. New York: Grand Central Publishing, 2016.

Parks, Stan and Coles, Dave. *24:14 - A Testimony to All Peoples*. Spring, TX: Self-published, 2019.

Patterson, George and Scoggins, Richard. *Church Multiplication Guide.* Rev. ed. Pasadena, CA: William Carey Library, 2001.

Shannon, Jennifer. *Don't Feed the Monkey Mind.* New Harbinger Publications, 2017.

Simpson, Wolfgang. *Houses that Change the World.* Authentic Media, 2001.

Sinclair, Daniel. *A Vision of the Possible: Pioneer Church Planting in Teams.* Downers Grove, IL. InterVarsity Press. 2005.

Sleeth, Matthew. *24/6: A Prescription for a Healthier, Happier Life.* Tyndale House Publishers, 2012.

Strauch, Alexander. *Biblical Eldership: An Urgent Call to Restore Biblical Church Leadership.* Littleton, CO: Lewis & Roth Publishers, 1988.

Subbamma, B.V. *New Patterns for Discipling Hindus.* Pasadena, CA: William Carey Library, 1970.

Thompson, Curt. *Anatomy of the Soul: Surprising Connections between Neuroscience and Spiritual Practices That Can Transform Your Life and Relationships.* Tyndale Momentum, 2010.

Tolle, Eckhart. *The Power of Now: A Guide to Spiritual Enlightenment.* New World Library, 2004.

Travis, John. "Messianic Muslim Followers of Isa: A Closer Look at C5 Believers and Congregations." *International Journal of Frontier Missions*, 17(1):2000 53-59.

Travis, John. "Must All Muslims Leave Islam to Follow Jesus?" *Evangelical Missions Quarterly*, 34(4): 1998, 411-415.

Travis, John. "The C1-C6 Spectrum." *Evangelical Missions Quarterly*, 34(4):1998,407-408.

Trousdale, Jerry. *Miraculous Movements.* Nashville TN: Thomas Nelson Publishing, 2012.

Warren, Rick. *The Purpose Driven Church*. Grand Rapids, MI: Zondervan Publishing House, 1995.

Warren, Rick. *The Purpose Driven Life: What on Earth Am I Here For?* Zondervan, 2012.

Watson, David and Watson, Paul. *Contagious Disciple Making: Leading Others on a Journey of Discovery*. Nashville TN: Thomas Nelson Publishing, 2014.

Woodbury, J. Dudley, ed. *From Seed to Fruit: Global Trends, Fruitful Practices, and Emerging Issues Among Muslims*. William Carey Library, 2008.

SPECIAL THANKS

This book has not been a one-person production. All along the way I tended to put it aside, waiting for a rainy day, in order not to have to work hard on a long-term project. The Lord always brought in friends to say, "Dan, how is the book going? Come on, we need to get it out there!"

Thank you to the wonderful endorsers and all your kind blurbs for the cover and inside pages. Several also gave very valuable input toward the final product. Thanks!

Mission: Possible has benefitted from lots of cooks in the kitchen, in a good way, i.e. friends who were happy to spend time with each chapter and point out the mistakes, flaws, and many bits that didn't make sense at first. Hopefully, most of those have been rectified. So I am very grateful for the star editing team God has given me. Particular thanks to A.T., Dick Brogden, K.C., Greg Livingstone, and my wife, Liz. Thank you Hannah Hakes for two very clear and helpful figures about movements. And the brass ring goes to Denele Ivins, who is actually an editor by profession, who gave up countless hours to bring this work to a higher level. So any remaining problems with logic or fact are their fault. Ha ha. Just kidding. No, those would be mine.

SPECIAL THANKS

Appendices 1 and 7 are significant contributions. So a big shout out to Stan Parks, Dave Coles, and Justin Long for the 24:14 / *Movements* piece, and to Anna Travis for *The Story of Alma*.

Many thanks to Wes Thiessen who helped it all come together, to get it produced and out the door. His professional completion work afforded the flexibility of self-publishing combined with the advantages of professional production and well-planned marketing.

Liz has been a consistent encouragement to keep writing, and her inputs to every chapter have been invaluable.

www.ingramcontent.com/pod-product-compliance
Lightning Source LLC
Chambersburg PA
CBHW070549010526
44118CB00012B/1273